THE CAROB

A fascinating collection of powder, the healthy alterna   ocolate.

THE
CAROB COOKBOOK

by

LORRAINE WHITESIDE
Illustrated by Ian Jones

THORSONS PUBLISHERS LIMITED
Wellingborough, Northamptonshire

First published 1981
This edition revised, enlarged and reset 1984

British Library Cataloguing in Publication Data

Whiteside, Lorraine
    The carob cookbook
    1. Cookery (Carob)
    I. Title
    641.6'446   TX813.C3

ISBN 0-7225-0907-3

Printed and bound in Great Britain

CONTENTS

PREFACE

Interest in natural food is increasing along with a growing awareness and acceptance of the importance of good nutrition in ensuring a healthy body and mind for life. Whilst a young person may have boundless vitality and energy on a junk food diet, in twenty years time that same person may well turn out to be a very unfit middle-aged individual.

Basing our diet on natural, unrefined foods is in all probability one of the most sensible and effective measures against ill health that we may ever take. As youngsters we give little thought to health and nutrition – our carefree lives are spent expending that seemingly infinite energy that we are naturally born with. But as the years pass we begin to realize that taking care of ourselves, becoming aware of how our bodies work and taking an interest in the foods we eat, is rewarding and above all necessary if we are to enjoy a long and illness-free existence.

Unfortunately, the majority of us spend some part of our lives abusing our bodies by eating and drinking too much of the wrong kind of things. Many people, albeit unknowingly, abuse their bodies throughout their entire lifetime.

The outstanding development of food technology that has taken place in this century has given us packaged convenience foods, a whole array of tinned foods with their chemical preservatives and even so-called 'fun foods' that are marketed and commercialized with little regard for the long-term effects on our health. The awful legacy of all this is that a lifetime of poor nutrition is endured by many of us, with an inevitable increased susceptibility to troublesome illnesses and degenerative diseases.

Thankfully, most caring and health-orientated people now realize that many foods that have in the past been labelled 'pure', such as white sugar and white flour, are empty foods with little or no nutritive value. The trend is now towards turning back to Mother Nature, eating the natural foods of the earth and renouncing the refining and preservation processes that are the product of a so-called civilized society. Ironically, in the case of food products, civilization has bred destruction.

Carob is one of the many health foods that is enjoying increasing popularity. Although it has been eaten by man for centuries, it has only recently been used as an alternative to chocolate. Unfortunately, the disadvantages of chocolate and cocoa consumption are little publicized and I am sure that many parents are unaware of the possible harm that an excessive intake of chocolate may be doing to their children, or the effect that it may be having on their behaviour. Fortunately, a healthy alternative to chocolate can now be offered to children and adults alike, one which I am sure will go on rising in popularity as junk foods fall from favour and natural wholefoods take their rightful place in human nutrition.

INTRODUCTION

Chocolate is one of the products that is all too often overlooked in a wholefooder's diet. On the premise that 'a little bit of what you fancy does you good', chocolate is consumed as a treat, a small 'won't-do-me-any-harm' indulgence, a nightly reward for keeping to a calorie-controlled diet, a soother and comforter.

For some, chocolate holds the same addictive properties that alcohol has for alcoholics – a passion that is indulged in often with the utmost secrecy. For others it is a psychological pick-me-up eaten during depression and emotionally disturbed moments, often as a substitute for love and affection.

In spite of the fact that many of us consider eating chocolate a 'sin', we nevertheless continue to consume it, as a nation, in large quantities, regardless of its alleged association with migraine, obesity, acne, tooth decay, diabetes and coronary diseases. So great is our love affair with chocolate that we conveniently choose to forget about the harmful reactions that it can produce in our bodies.

Chocolate's Methylxanthine Content
Most people are aware that chocolate is produced from the cocoa bean, but what is not generally known is that both chocolate and cocoa contain caffeine and theobromine, both chemical substances that are classed as methylxanthines. Theophylline, which is present in tea,

is also classed as a methylxanthine.

Methylxanthines stimulate both the central nervous system and the cardiovascular system, increase the amount of gastric acid that is secreted in the stomach and have a diuretic effect on the kidneys. To put it more plainly, the caffeine and theobromine contained in chocolate and cocoa can play havoc with your nerves, make your heart beat faster and give you an upset stomach.

Research that has recently been carried out indicates that mothers who breast-feed their babies should eliminate chocolate from their diet during the nursing period. This is because caffeine and theobromine are passed onto the baby through the mother's milk, producing a certain amount of hyperactivity and a proneness to diarrhoea, eczema and constipation.

A link has also been discovered between fibrocystic breast disease – a condition characterized by fibrous tissue and cyst fluid in the breast – and consumption of methylxanthines such as those found in chocolate, cocoa, coffee, tea and cola drinks. Dr John Minton's extensive research on this female disorder led him to discover that 47 women who were suffering from this disease all consumed, on average, 190 mg of methylxanthines each day. Most of the women who eliminated all sources of methylxanthines from their diet found that the condition disappeared completely within two months to one year.

Chocolate's Allergenic Properties
Chocolate is one of the most common allergens, capable of triggering off headaches, migraine, depression, mental confusion, anxiety, panic attacks, hyperactivity, even hallucinations and violent behaviour. Some other common allergens are eggs, wheat, cow's milk, sugar, coffee, to name but a few.

In his book *Not all in the Mind* (Pan, 1976), the leading British allergy expert, Dr Richard Mackarness, puts forward his belief that food and chemical allergies may be responsible for disorders of the respiratory system, the skin, the digestive system, the cardiovascular system, the musculo-skeletal system, the central nervous system, the genito-urinary system, the mind and the endocrine system. Dr Mackarness also says that 30 per cent of people seeking medical attention show symptoms that are directly related to a food or chemical allergy.

Dr Arthur Coca, who pioneered allergy research in the United States, is convinced that 90 per cent of the population is likely to suffer from food allergies. A survey carried out by Dr Coca amongst 100 patients demonstrated that 17 out of the group were allergic to chocolate. The most common allergy was to eggs, with 33 of the patients showing allergic reactions.

One of the major causes for concern is that a lot of allergies go undetected. Many individuals are inclined to relate the unpleasant symptoms to other disorders, not suspecting that they may be suffering from an intolerance to one or several types of food. Fatigue, irritability, palpitations or other unusual symptoms are indicative of a possible food allergy.

If you would like to find out if you are allergic to chocolate or any other foodstuffs, try the pulse test put forward by Dr Coca in his book *The Pulse Test – Easy Allergy Detection*.* As the pulse rate is believed to speed up after consuming a food allergen, Dr Coca suggests that the pulse be taken on waking and at periodic intervals during the day, particularly after eating. In Dr Coca's estimation, a pulse rate of more than 84 beats per minute could be produced by an allergic reaction.

If you notice any unpleasant symptoms after eating chocolate or drinking cocoa and have a noticeably increased pulse rate, the chances are that you are allergic to them.

Chocolate's Oxalic Acid Content

Although there is calcium in the cocoa bean, a significant amount of oxalic acid is also present, which renders the

* Distributed in the U.K. by Thorsons.

calcium unavailable to the body. When calcium combines with oxalic acid during digestion, it forms calcium oxalate, an insoluble compound that is incapable of being absorbed by the body. Thus calcium that is consumed in conjunction with oxalic acid passes through the system without being assimilated. Because of this, when cocoa or drinking chocolate is added to milk, the nutritive value of the calcium normally obtained when the milk is drunk alone, is destroyed.

Carob, the Healthy Alternative
Delectable though chocolate may be, its nutritional disadvantages combined with the potentially harmful allergic reactions and stimulating effects that it produces have given rise to the need for a harmless, yet equally delicious alternative. Carob has been found to be that alternative.

Carob has enjoyed recognition in health food circles in the United States for some years and its popularity in the United Kingdom is increasing along with the growing demand for natural foods and the awareness that a healthy diet is reflected in a healthy body and mind. In the same way that honey and molasses are being used in place of refined sugar, wholemeal flour instead of white and fresh, additive-free foods instead of tinned and processed items, now chocolate, which has impassioned so many of us for so long, has a substitute.

The Carob Tree and its Origin
The carob tree (Ceratonia siliqua) originated in the Middle East and later spread to countries bordering the Mediterranean Sea such as Italy, Spain, Morocco, Greece and Cyprus. The tree flourishes in these warm climates and in many areas it grows uncultivated. The carob tree was introduced into the United States about a century ago and is grown in southern regions where the climate is similar to that of the Mediterranean countries.

The carob tree is a large evergreen which bears glossy brown edible seed pods which grow to about 4-12 inches (10-30 cm) in length and 1-2 inches (2.5-5 cm) in width, and contain a sweet-tasting edible pulp. Although the tree takes about 50 years to reach its fully grown height of 40-50 feet (12-15 m) and only begins to yield fruit on a regular basis after 15 years, it lives to a very great age and will go on producing fruit for many years.

The fruit is also known as the 'locust bean', or 'St John's Bread' as the pods were said to have provided nourishment for St John the Baptist in the wilderness. It is also said that the husks or pods were the food on which the prodigal son survived.

The carob fruit has for centuries been considered a valuable source of nourishment for man and beast, and the hard seeds that nestle within the pods were once used by goldsmiths and jewellers as a standard for measuring the weight of gold and precious stones. Indeed, the word 'carat', still in use today, is derived from the name given to the seeds of the carob fruit.

How Carob Powder is Made

Carob powder is made from carefully selected pods of the carob tree which are washed to remove any foreign bodies. The pulp is then separated from the pod by means of a coarse-grinding process, after which the pulp is sieved, roasted and blended into a fine powder which is similar in flavour and texture to cocoa powder.

Carob's Nutritional Advantages

The nutritional advantages of carob must inevitably be compared with the disadvantages of chocolate, although far from being just a substitute, carob is a nutritive food in its own right. Carob powder's 8 per cent protein content is relatively high when compared with other vegetable products. It is also a good source of vitamins A, D, B_1 (thiamin), B_2 (riboflavin) and B_3 (niacin). Carob,

in fact, provides as much thiamin as asparagus or strawberries, its riboflavin content is equivalent to that of
brown rice and it contains as much niacin as lima beans or
dates. Good quantities of several important minerals are
also present, including calcium, magnesium and potassium,
as well as the trace minerals iron, manganese, barium,
chromium, copper and nickel. It is little wonder with its
high nutritive value that the carob tree is also known as
the 'Tree of life'.

When carob is compared with chocolate, its advantages
become very clear. To begin with, carob contains no
caffeine or theobromine, the harmful substances which,
as mentioned, may produce several undesirable reactions
in our systems. It has none of the allergenic properties
associated with chocolate and cocoa. Nor does it contain
any oxalic acid, the substance that renders calcium
unavailable to the body. Furthermore, carob powder
contains less fat and less sodium than cocoa powder and
has a higher crude fibre content. As it is made up of
approximately 46 per cent natural sugars, including
fructose, carob requires less sweetening than chocolate
or cocoa powder.

Medicinal Value of Carob's Pectin Content

Carob's principal medicinal value lies in its high pectin
content, a gelatinous water-soluble substance which
occurs naturally in fruits on ripening and which is used as
a gelling agent in jams and jellies. Pectin is particularly
valuable for regulating the digestion and protecting the
body naturally against diarrhoea.

Carob powder has been used successfully in the United
States, Canada and Europe in the prevention and treatment
of diarrhoea in children, when the condition is caused
specifically by a digestive upset, heat or fatigue rather
than by a germ or as a result of a more serious complaint.
Digestive disorders such as this are fairly recurrent in
young children and are particularly distressing for the

parents. Experiments with carob powder have produced good results when given to children at a 5 per cent concentration, that is one tablespoonful to 8 fl oz (225 ml) of warm milk. In most cases the disorder cleared up within approximately 24 hours. Reports of such experiments have been published in the Journal of the Canadian Medical Association and the U.S. *Journal of Pediatrics*.

Carob also contains lignin, which like pectin, is recognized as a digestion regulator and for its protective properties against diarrhoea, particularly in children.

Other Medicinal Values
The Carob fruit is also highly valued in the Middle East and Asia for its medicinal properties. In the Middle East a decoction of the fruit is made and the water in which it has been boiled is drunk to relieve catarrhal infections. In Asia, particularly India, the pods are known for their astringent properties and are used to counteract coughs.

Is Carob Fattening?
Like all sweet things, carob can be fattening when taken in excess but compared with chocolate or cocoa it has a much lower calorie content. One hundred grams of cocoa powder will add 295 calories to your diet whereas the same amount of carob powder rates only 177 calories. So, for those of us who need to watch our weight yet find it difficult to resist the temptation of a little bit of sweetness, carob will do less damage to the waistline than chocolate. With its lower calorie content, carob can be more easily incorporated into a 1,000-calorie-a-day diet, and you can rest in the knowledge that your 'once-a-day-treat' is far more than just junk food.

How to Use Carob
Carob powder can be used in any recipe as a substitute for cocoa powder. Its distinctive chocolate-like flavour combines well with fresh and dried fruits, nuts, honey and

yogurt, and it can be used in endless ways to make delicious, nutritious cakes, biscuits and desserts.

Carob is also available in block form, just like a bar of chocolate and is without doubt a firm favourite with the children. It can be melted over hot water to be added to your recipes or to make a delicious sauce. Also, it can be bought in the form of an instant beverage which can be made into a night-cap just by adding hot milk or water.

A Word About the Other Ingredients

Wholemeal Flour
If the health of your family is your main concern, you should not consider using anything but 100 per cent wholemeal flour for all your baking. It is a vital part of healthy eating, providing an excellent source of fibre, and is the richest known source of vitamin E. It also contains significant amounts of the B vitamins and protein.

Wholemeal flour is, of course, much coarser in texture than white flour, and you may at first find it more difficult to handle. But you can be certain that your family will applaud the improved flavour of cakes, teabreads, biscuits, puddings and pastries made with wholemeal flour.

Polyunsaturated Margarine
The fat ingredient used in all the recipes is polyunsaturated margarine. This is by personal choice and you may, of course, prefer to use butter. However, there has been much research into the causes of atherosclerosis (a condition resulting from fatty substances being deposited on the arterial walls) and it is evident that one of the major causes is the intake of a high proportion of saturated fats. These fatty deposits may produce partial blockages, thickening the arterial wall and thus narrowing the size of the channel through which the blood passes. In advanced cases strokes or coronary occlusions may result.

Saturated fats can be recognized by their solidity at room temperature – butter, lard and meat fat for example. Unsaturated fats on the other hand are liquid fats derived from vegetables and cereals. Oils which are highest in polyunsaturates are safflower, sunflower, soya, corn and wheat germ. One of the principal values of vegetable oils is their high linoleic acid content which is needed by the body before particles of fat can be broken down and utilized.

Both the United Kingdom Medical Research Council and the United States Senate Select Committee have advised the public to reduce their saturated fat intake and there would seem to be little doubt that increased usage of unsaturated fats is a sensible measure to take in the prevention of ill health.

The most popular polyunsaturated margarines are those made from sunflower and corn oils. These are ideal for baking, particularly if your aim is to reduce the proportion of saturated fats consumed by your family.

Raw Cane Sugar
In many countries, the purer and whiter the sugar, the better it is believed to be, but no belief could be more erroneous. The sugar refining process removes all the valuable vitamins and minerals, leaving an end-product that is pure carbohydrate and totally devoid of nutrients.

The residue that remains when the sugar refining process is completed is known as molasses and until recently it was only thought to be fit for animal consumption, but it has at last been justly recognized as a valuable source of vitamins and minerals in human nutrition. Molasses is a particularly good source of the B vitamins and is rich in iron, copper, calcium, phosphorus and potassium.

Raw cane sugar contains varying degrees of molasses and, generally speaking, the darker the sugar, the greater its nutritional value, as the colour of the sugar indicates the amount of molasses it contains. A very dark, almost black sugar therefore has a higher proportion of molasses than a lighter-coloured sugar.

However, not all brown sugar is natural raw cane sugar. Certain types of so-called 'brown' sugar are simply white sugar that has been coloured. The way to check whether brown sugar is genuine raw cane sugar or not is to put a spoonful into a glass of water and if it turns white as it sinks to the bottom, it is not. To be absolutely sure that you are buying genuine raw cane sugar, always choose brands which state the country of origin on the packet and wherever possible buy your sugar from health food stores where you will find genuine Muscovado and Barbados sugars.

Honey
Renowned for its curative and healing properties, honey has been used by man throughout the ages. The prophet Mohammed said: 'Honey is a remedy for all ills', and Solomon's advice was: 'My son, eat thou honey for it is good'. The ancient Egyptians applied honey to burns and wounds and used it as a sacrificial offering to their gods.

Honey is in fact one of the most pure sources of natural sugars. It is particularly valuable as a source of energy because the principal sugars that it contains – levulose (fructose) and dextrose (glucose) – are rapidly assimilated by the body and thus quickly converted into energy.

Honey contains vitamins A, B_1, B_2, B_3, pantothenic acid, B_6, biotin, folic acid and vitamin C, and there are traces of iron, copper, sodium, potassium, calcium, magnesium, phosphorus and manganese. Honey also contains a substance known as acetylcholine which helps to increase the flow of blood to the heart whilst decreasing the blood pressure and the heart rate at the same time.

As a substitute for sugar, honey is second to none. It gives extra flavour and goodness to cakes, biscuits, puddings, hot and cold drinks – in fact any recipes in which sugar is required. You will also find that cakes stay fresh longer when honey is added owing to the increased moisture, but biscuits may lose their crispness, so unless you plan to eat them on the day that they are made, it is probably wiser to stick to raw cane sugar so that they don't become soft during storage.

Yogurt

According to an ancient Persian tradition, an angel revealed the secret of making yogurt to the prophet Abraham and to this he owed his long life and fertility. We are told in the Bible that he reached the age of 175 and became the father of a child when he was 100 years old.

Yogurt is as valued a food today as it was in ancient times. It is rich in protein, calcium and the B vitamins, and it contains health-giving bacteria known as *Lactobacillus bulgaricus* which promote the growth of other beneficial bacteria in the intestinal tract. Sufferers from digestive complaints often find yogurt helps them through its stabilizing influence on the normal lactic flora in the intestine. As it does not have the same allergenic properties that milk has, people who suffer from milk intolerance are able to take yogurt without any trouble.

Yogurt has a very significant role in a healthy eating programme and as it combines well with most foods, it can be incorporated into almost any recipe. Added to cakes, puddings, and biscuits, yogurt provides extra protein and vitamins, improved flavour and increased moisture. It can be used in place of cream and as a protein alternative to eggs.

Always choose natural, unsweetened yogurt as many of the flavoured yogurts contain preservatives, colouring and refined sugar.

Comparison of Carob Powder with Cocoa Powder
(based on a typical analysis)

	Carob Powder	Cocoa Powder
Calories per 100g	177	295
Crude Fat	0.7%	23.7%
Carbohydrates:		
Natural Sugars	46.0%	5.5%
Crude Fibre	7.0%	4.3%
Other Carbohydrates		
(by difference)	35.4%	38.5%
Crude Protein	4.5%	16.8%
Ash	3.4%	8.2%
Moisture	3.0%	3.0%
Iron (mg/100g)	50	10
Sodium (mg/100g)	100	700
Potassium (mg/100g)	950	650
Caffeine	Nil	0.16%
Theobromine	Nil	1.1%

The above table kindly supplied by Granary Foods Ltd
of Burton-on-Trent.

1.

EVERYDAY CAKES AND TEABREADS

Although the majority of commercially sold cakes made with refined flour and refined sugar are of little nutritive value, cakes made at home with 100 per cent wholemeal flour, raw cane sugar and other natural ingredients can play a significant part in a wholefood diet, providing the body with unrefined carbohydrate and fibre.

As a substitute for chocolate and cocoa powder, carob is the perfect ingredient for wholemeal cakes, giving a delicious flavour and that very special 'chocolate appeal'.

In cakes, biscuits and gâteaux, carob's distinctive flavour is enhanced by combining it with the added flavours of orange and vanilla, and this harmonious combination of flavours is reflected throughout the book.

A melted carob bar makes an ideal coating for sponge cakes and teabreads, giving them a dark and delicious, glossy finish and adding a natural, ever-appealing 'chocolate' flavour.

CAROB SWISS ROLL
Serves 6

A Swiss roll always makes a welcome sight on a tea-time table. Here the carob and vanilla flavoured roll encases an orange custard filling; the custard-filled roll is then fully masked with a dark and glossy carob coating.

Imperial (Metric)	American
4 eggs	4 eggs
4 oz (115g) Vanilla Sugar (page 189)	⅔ cupsful Vanilla Sugar (page 189)
3½ oz (100g) wholemeal flour	¾ cupful + 1 tablespoonful wholewheat flour
¾ oz (20g) carob powder	2 tablespoonsful carob powder
¾ oz (20g) polyunsaturated margarine, melted and cooled	2 tablespoonsful polyunsaturated margarine, melted and cooled

Filling:	*Filling:*
Orange Custard Filling (page 178)	Orange Custard Filling (page 178)

Coating and Decoration:	*Coating and Decoration:*
Plain Carob Coating (page 183)	Plain Carob Coating (page 183)
Quartered orange slices	Quartered orange slices
Small fresh flowers	Small fresh flowers

1. Whisk the eggs and vanilla sugar together until thick, creamy and tripled in volume. (The whisk should leave a distinct trail when lifted from the mixture.)

2. Carefully fold the flour and carob powder into the egg mixture, adding alternately with the melted margarine. Incorporate the ingredients as lightly and as quickly as possible, so that the mixture retains as much of its volume as possible, resulting in a really light cake.

3. Pour the mixture into a Swiss roll tin measuring

approximately 9 x 13 inches (23 x 33cm), and lined with greased greaseproof paper. Spread the mixture evenly with a palette knife, then bake at 400°F/200°C (Gas Mark 6) for about 12 minutes, until firm and springy to the touch.

4. Lay a piece of greaseproof paper on a flat surface. Turn the sponge onto the greaseproof paper and peel off the lining paper. Trim the crusty edges off the sponge, then lay a second piece of greaseproof paper on top. Carefully roll up the sponge, with the greaseproof paper inside.

5. When the sponge has cooled, unroll and discard the greaseproof paper. Spread the prepared orange custard filling over the sponge, then re-roll.

6. Spoon the Carob Coating over the custard-filled roll, covering completely, then set aside to allow the coating to set. Decorate the top of the roll with some quartered orange slices, interspaced with some small fresh flowers. Decorate around the base of the roll with some additional orange slices and small flowers.

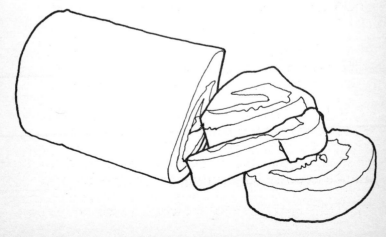

CAROB COATED APPLE CAKE

Two layers of wholemeal sponge cake, dotted with hazelnuts, are sandwiched together with an apple purée and topped with a dark carob coating.

Imperial (Metric)
4 oz (115 g) polyunsaturated margarine
3 oz (85 g) raw cane sugar
1 oz (30 g) Vanilla Sugar (page 189)
2 eggs, lightly beaten
2 oz (55 g) chopped hazelnuts
4 oz (115 g) wholemeal flour
1½ teaspoonsful baking powder

Filling:
1 lb (455 g) dessert apples (Golden Delicious or similar juicy variety)
Finely grated zest and juice of ½ lemon
1 oz (30 g) raw cane sugar

Coating and Decoration:
Plain Carob Coating (page 183)
12 whole hazelnuts

American
½ cupful polyunsaturated margarine
½ cupful raw cane sugar
2 tablespoonsful Vanilla Sugar (page 189)
2 eggs, lightly beaten
½ cupful chopped hazelnuts
1 cupful wholewheat flour
1½ teaspoonsful baking powder

Filling:
4 medium dessert apples (Golden Delicious or similar juicy variety)
Finely grated zest and juice of ½ lemon
2 tablespoons raw cane sugar

Coating and Decoration:
Plain Carob Coating (page 183)
12 whole hazelnuts

1. To make the hazelnut sponge, cream the margarine, raw cane sugar and vanilla sugar together until pale and creamy.

2. Gradually add the beaten eggs, then incorporate the chopped hazelnuts.

3. Fold in the flour and baking powder, then spoon the mixture into a greased 8 inch (20 cm) round cake tin. Bake at 350°F/180°C (Gas Mark 4) for 25-30 minutes,

until nicely risen and firm to the touch.

4. Meanwhile, make the apple purée. Peel and core the fruit, then slice into a saucepan, together with the lemon zest, lemon juice and raw cane sugar. Cook over a low heat until the fruit is reduced to a soft pulp. Using a fork, blend the apples to a smooth purée, then set aside to cool.

5. When cool, slice the hazelnut sponge in half and sandwich together with the apple purée. Spread the Carob Coating over the top of the cake and complete by decorating with some whole hazelnuts.

CAROB AND ORANGE SOURED CREAM CAKE

Serves 6-8

This melt-in-the-mouth carob cake is flavoured with orange zest and sandwiched together with a soured cream filling.

Imperial (Metric)	American
4 eggs	4 eggs
3 oz (85g) Vanilla Sugar (page 189)	½ cupful Vanilla Sugar (page 189)
Finely grated zest of 1 orange	Finely grated zest of 1 orange
3 oz (85g) wholemeal flour	¾ cupful wholewheat flour
¾ oz (20g) carob powder	2 tablespoonsful carob powder
¾ oz (20g) polyunsaturated margarine, melted and cooled	2 tablespoonsful polyunsaturated margarine, melted and cooled

Filling and Decoration:	*Filling and Decoration:*
Soured Cream Filling (page 182)	Soured Cream Filling (page 182)
Quartered orange slices	Quartered orange slices
Toasted almonds	Toasted almonds

1. Place the eggs, vanilla sugar and grated orange zest in a mixing bowl and beat until thick, creamy and tripled in volume. (The whisk should leave a distinct trail when lifted from the mixture.)

2. Mix the flour and carob powder together, then carefully fold into the mixture, adding alternately with the melted margarine. Incorporate the ingredients as lightly as possible so that the mixture retains its maximum volume.

3. Pour the mixture into a Swiss roll tin measuring approximately 9 x 13 inches (23 x 33cm), lined with greased greaseproof paper. Spread the mixture evenly

with a palette knife, then bake at 400°F/200°C (Gas Mark 6) for about 12 minutes, until the cake is firm and springy to the touch.

4. When cool, turn the carob cake out of the tin and peel off the lining paper. Trim the crusty edges off the cake, then cut crossways into three equally-sized rectangles.

5. Sandwich the three layers together with the Soured Cream Filling, and spread a thin coating of the filling over the top layer of the cake.

6. Complete the cake by decorating with some quartered orange slices and some toasted almonds. If you wish, dot the cake with two small fresh flowers, to add a splash of colour to the decoration.

CAROB COATED PECAN AND BANANA BREAD

Makes a 2lb (900g) loaf cake

A dark carob coating combines particularly well with the flavour of this popular fruit and nut teabread.

Imperial (Metric)	American
5 oz (140g) polyunsaturated margarine	½ cupful + 2½ tablespoonsful polyunsaturated margarine
5 oz (140g) Vanilla Sugar (page 189)	⅔ cupful + 2 tablespoonsful Vanilla Sugar (page 189)
3 eggs, lightly beaten	3 eggs, lightly beaten
3 bananas	3 bananas
10 oz (285g) wholemeal flour	2½ cupsful wholewheat flour
2½ teaspoonsful baking powder	2½ teaspoonsful baking powder
4 oz (115g) pecans, chopped	¾ cupful pecans, chopped
1 tablespoon natural yogurt or milk	1 tablespoonful natural yogurt or milk

Coating and Decoration:	*Coating and Decoration:*
Plain Carob Coating (page 183)	Plain Carob Coating (page 183)
8 whole pecan nuts	8 whole pecan nuts

1. Cream the margarine and Vanilla Sugar together until pale and fluffy.

2. Gradually incorporate the beaten eggs, adding a little at a time.

3. Peel the bananas and mash to a smooth purée with a fork. Fold the banana purée into the creamed mixture.

4. Now fold in the flour, baking powder, pecans and natural yogurt or milk, blending all the ingredients to a soft dropping consistency.

5. Spoon the mixture into a greased 2lb (900g) loaf tin, smoothing over the top, then bake at 350°F/180°C (Gas Mark 4) for about 1¼ hours, until well risen and firm to the touch. Test the teabread by inserting a fine skewer into it; if the skewer comes out clean, the teabread is cooked through.

6. Allow the teabread to cool thoroughly, then spread the Carob Coating on top, allowing some of it to drizzle down the sides of the teabread. Complete by decorating with some whole pecan nuts.

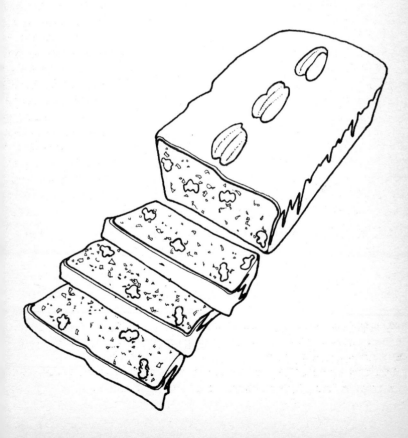

CAROB MANDARIN AND ALMOND CAKE

Serves 8

The flavourful and fragrant zest and juice of mandarin oranges penetrate this delicious almond-masked carob cake.

Imperial (Metric)
6 eggs, separated
5 oz (140g) raw cane sugar
Finely grated zest of 2
    mandarin oranges
Strained juice of 1 mandarin
    orange
3½ oz (100g) wholemeal flour
2 oz (55g) ground almonds
¾ oz (20g) carob powder

American
6 eggs, separated
⅔ cupful + 2 tablespoonsful
    raw cane sugar
Finely grated zest of 2
    mandarin oranges
Strained juice of 1 mandarin
    orange
¾ cupful + 1 tablespoonful
    wholewheat flour
½ cupful ground almonds
2 tablespoonsful carob powder

Coating and Decoration:
2 tablespoonsful raw cane
    sugar apricot jam
1 tablespoonful water
4 oz (115g) flaked almonds,
    lightly toasted
12 mandarin orange segments,
    pith and segment membrane
    removed
Fresh flower

Coating and Decoration:
2 tablespoonsful raw cane
    sugar apricot jelly
1 tablespoonful water
1 cupful slivered almonds,
    lightly toasted
12 mandarin orange segments,
    pith and segment membrane
    removed
Fresh flower

1. Place the egg yolks, sugar and orange zest in a mixing bowl and whisk until the mixture lightens and becomes thick and creamy. When the mixture reaches this consistency, whisk in the orange juice.

2. Mix the flour, ground almonds and carob powder together, combining them well.

3. In a separate bowl, whisk the egg whites until they stand in stiff peaks, then carefully fold into the egg yolk mixture, incorporating alternately with the dry ingredients, and beginning and ending with the whisked egg whites. Fold in the ingredients as carefully and as lightly as possible, so that the egg whites retain as much of their volume as possible, resulting in a meltingly light cake.

4. Pour the mixture into a greased 9 inch (23cm) round, deep cake tin and bake at 375°F/190°C (Gas Mark 5) for 35-40 minutes, until the cake is well risen and firm and springy to the touch.

5. Allow the cake to cool thoroughly, then melt the apricot jam and water together in a saucepan set over a moderate heat. Brush the melted jam all over the top and sides of the cake, then cover the cake straight away with the lightly toasted almonds, compressing the nuts gently with the hands to ensure that they remain firmly secured on the top and sides of the cake.

6. Decorate the outer edge of the cake with a circle of orange segments, and complete by placing a brightly coloured fresh flower, preferably of an exotic appearance, in the centre of the cake.

JAVANESE SPICE CAKE

Makes one 2lb (900g) loaf cake

Dark, spicy and full of flavour and goodness.

Imperial (Metric)	American
9 oz (255 g) wholemeal flour	2¼ cupsful wholewheat flour
2 oz (55g) fine oatmeal	½ cupful fine oatmeal
2 teaspoonsful ground cinnamon	2 teaspoonsful ground cinnamon
1 teaspoonful mixed spice	1 teaspoonful mixed spice
1 teaspoonful ground ginger	1 teaspoonful ground ginger
1 teaspoonful bicarbonate of soda	1 teaspoonful bicarbonate of soda
1 oz (30g) carob powder	¼ cupful carob powder
4 oz (115g) light Muscovado sugar	⅔ cupful light Muscovado sugar
6 oz (170g) polyunsaturated margarine	¾ cupful polyunsaturated margarine
2 tablespoonsful molasses	2 tablespoonsful molasses
2 eggs, lightly beaten	2 eggs, lightly beaten
2 tablespoonsful natural yogurt	2 tablespoonsful natural yogurt

Topping and Decoration:	*Topping and Decoration:*
Orange Butter Cream (page 182)	Orange Butter Cream (page 182)
Quartered orange slices	Quartered orange slices
Whole pecans	Whole pecans

1. Place the flour, oatmeal, spices, bicarbonate of soda, carob powder and Muscovado sugar in a mixing bowl, combining them well.

2. Melt the margarine and molasses together in a saucepan set over a moderate heat.

3. Make a well in the centre of the dry ingredients, then pour in the melted margarine and molasses, and the beaten eggs. Begin blending the ingredients together,

adding sufficient natural yogurt to give a soft dropping consistency.

4. Spoon the mixture into a greased 2 lb (900g) loaf tin, smoothing over the top, then bake at 325°F/170°C (Gas Mark 3) for 1¼-1½ hours, until firm to the touch. Test the cake by inserting a fine skewer into it; if the skewer comes out clean, the cake is cooked through.

5. Allow to cool thoroughly, then spread the Orange Butter Cream on top of the cake. Decorate with some quartered orange slices and whole pecan nuts.

CAROB COATED PINEAPPLE CAKE

This wholemeal sponge cake is dotted with natural dried pineapple and topped with a flavour-contrasting carob coating.

Imperial (Metric)	American
6 oz (170g) polyunsaturated margarine	¾ cupful polyunsaturated margarine
6 oz (170g) raw cane sugar	1 cupful raw cane sugar
Finely grated zest of 1 orange	Finely grated zest of 1 orange
3 eggs, lightly beaten	3 eggs, lightly beaten
5 oz (140g) wholemeal flour	1¼ cupsful wholewheat flour
2 oz (55g) ground almonds	½ cupful ground almonds
2 teaspoonsful baking powder	2 teaspoonsful baking powder
4 oz (115g) dried pineapple, chopped	⅔ cupful dried pineapple, chopped
1-2 tablespoonsful milk	1-2 tablespoonsful milk

Coating and Decoration:
Plain Carob Coating (page 183)
4-6 chunks dried pineapple
12 split blanched almonds, lightly toasted

Coating and Decoration:
Plain Carob Coating (page 183)
4-6 chunks dried pineapple
12 split blanched almonds, lightly toasted

1. Cream the margarine, raw cane sugar and finely grated orange zest together until pale and fluffy.

2. Gradually incorporate the beaten eggs, adding a little at a time and beating well after each addition.

3. Now fold in the flour, ground almonds, baking powder and dried pineapple, adding a small quantity of milk to give a soft dropping consistency.

4. Spoon the mixture into a greased 8 inch (20cm) round, deep cake tin, smoothing over the top, then bake at 350°F/180°C (Gas Mark 4) for about 1 hour, or until the cake is nicely risen and firm to the touch. Test the cake

by inserting a fine skewer into it; if the skewer comes out clean, the cake is cooked through.

5. Turn out of the tin and allow to cool thoroughly, then spread the Carob Coating on top of the cake, allowing some of it to drizzle down the sides. Place a ring of pineapple chunks in the centre of the cake, to decorate, then place a circle of lightly toasted almonds around the outer edge of the cake, to complete the decoration.

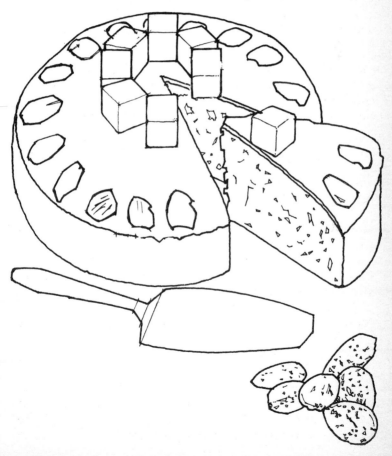

CAROB AND DATE TEABREAD

Makes a 1 lb (455g) loaf cake

Imperial (Metric)
6 oz (170g) wholemeal flour
2 teaspoonsful baking powder
3 oz (85g) polyunsaturated
   margarine
2 oz (55g) carob powder
6 oz (170g) dates, stoned
1 egg, lightly beaten
2 tablespoonsful clear honey
3 tablespoonsful natural yogurt
   or milk

Decoration:
10-12 whole pecans or walnuts
2 teaspoonsful clear honey

American
1½ cupsful wholewheat flour
2 teaspoonsful baking powder
⅓ cupful polyunsaturated
   margarine
½ cupful carob powder
1 cupful dates, stoned
1 egg, lightly beaten
2 tablespoonsful clear honey
3 tablespoonsful natural yogurt
   or milk

Decoration:
10-12 whole pecans or English
   walnuts
2 teaspoonsful clear honey

1. Combine the flour and baking powder in a mixing bowl.

2. Rub the margarine into the dry ingredients, using the fingertips, until a breadcrumb consistency is obtained, then fold in the carob powder.

3. Coarsely chop the dates and fold into the flour mixture, making sure that they are evenly distributed, as they tend to cling together in small clumps.

4. Make a well in the centre of the flour mixture and pour in the beaten egg and honey. Draw the flour over the well and begin blending the ingredients together, then add sufficient natural yogurt or milk to give a soft dropping consistency.

5. Spoon the mixture into a greased 1 lb (455g) loaf tin,

smoothing over the top, then bake at 350°F/180°C (Gas Mark 4) for about 1 hour, until firm to the touch.

6. Allow the teabread to cool, then decorate the top with some whole pecans or walnuts, secured by spreading the underside of the nuts with a little clear honey.

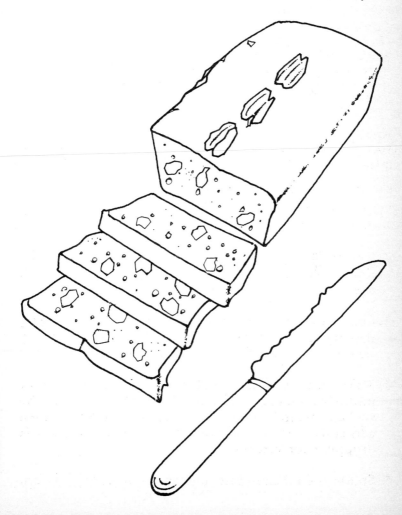

CAROB COATED ORANGE AND ALMOND RING

Serves 8-10

This attractive ring cake is flavoured with orange zest and almonds and topped with a dark and glossy carob coating.

Imperial (Metric)	American
5 eggs, separated	5 eggs, separated
4 oz (115g) raw cane sugar	⅔ cupful raw cane sugar
Finely grated zest of 1 orange	Finely grated zest of 1 orange
2½ oz (70g) wholemeal flour	⅔ cupful wholewheat flour
1½ oz (45g) ground almonds	½ cupful ground almonds

Coating and Decoration:	*Coating and Decoration:*
Plain Carob Coating (page 183)	Plain Carob Coating (page 183)
2 oz (55g) flaked almonds, lightly toasted	½ cupful slivered almonds, lightly toasted

1. Place the egg yolks, sugar and grated orange zest in a mixing bowl and whisk well until the mixture lightens and becomes thick and creamy.

2. In a separate bowl, whisk the egg whites until they stand in stiff peaks.

3. Mix the flour and ground almonds together, then carefully fold the whisked egg whites and dry ingredients into the egg yolk mixture, incorporating them alternately, beginning and ending with the egg whites. Fold in the ingredients as lightly as possible so that the whites retain their maximum volume, to give a meltingly light cake.

4. Pour the mixture into a well-greased ring mould, filling about three-quarters full, to allow room for the cake to rise whilst baking. Bake at 375°F/190°C (Gas Mark 5) for 30-35 minutes, until nicely risen and firm to the touch.

5. When the ring cake is cool, spread the Carob Coating on top, allowing some of it to drizzle down the sides of the cake. Sprinkle some lightly toasted flaked almonds on top of the Carob Coating and allow to set before serving.

CAROB WALNUT AND RAISIN TEABREAD

Makes one 1 lb (455g) loaf cake

Imperial (Metric)	American
6 oz (170g) polyunsaturated margarine	¾ cupful polyunsaturated margarine
4 oz (115g) raw cane sugar	⅔ cupful raw cane sugar
3 eggs, lightly beaten	3 eggs, lightly beaten
6 oz (170g) wholemeal flour	1½ cupsful wholewheat flour
1 oz (30g) carob powder	¼ cupful carob powder
2½ teaspoonsful baking powder	2½ teaspoonsful baking powder
3 oz (85g) walnuts, coarsely chopped	⅔ cupful English walnuts, coarsely chopped
3 oz (85g) small raisins	½ cupful small raisins
8 walnut halves	8 walnut halves

1. Cream the margarine and raw cane sugar together until light and fluffy.

2. Gradually incorporate the beaten eggs, adding a little at a time, then fold in the flour, carob powder and baking powder.

3. Fold in the walnuts and raisins, then spoon the mixture into a greased 1 lb (455g) loaf tin. Smooth over the top of the mixture and decorate with some walnut halves.

4. Bake the cake at 350°F/180°C (Gas Mark 4) for about 1 hour, until nicely risen and firm to the touch. Test the cake by inserting a fine skewer into it; if the skewer comes out clean, the cake is cooked through.

CAROB JAMAICAN RUM CAKE

Serves 6-8

Imperial (Metric)
4 eggs
4 oz (115 g) light Muscovado sugar
Finely grated zest of 1 orange
3½ oz (100 g) wholemeal flour
¾ oz (20 g) carob powder
¾ oz (20 g) ground almonds
2 tablespoonsful dark Jamaican rum

American
4 eggs
⅔ cupful light Muscovado sugar
Finely grated zest of 1 orange
¾ cupful + 1 tablespoonful wholewheat flour
2 tablespoonsful carob powder
2 tablespoonsful ground almonds
2 tablespoonsful dark Jamaican rum

Filling and Topping:
Vanilla Custard Filling (page 177)
2 tablespoonsful pure maple syrup
1 oz (30 g) desiccated coconut
Small fresh flower

Filling and Topping:
Vanilla Custard Filling (page 177)
2 tablespoonsful pure maple syrup
⅓ cupful desiccated coconut
Small fresh flower

1. Place the eggs, sugar and orange zest in a mixing bowl and whisk until thick, creamy and tripled in volume. (The whisk should leave a distinct trail when lifted from the mixture.)

2. Mix the flour, carob powder and ground almonds together, combining them well, then carefully fold into the egg mixture, adding alternately with the Jamaican rum.

3. Pour the mixture into a greased 8 inch (20 cm) round, deep cake tin and bake at 375°F/190°C (Gas Mark 5) for 30-35 minutes, until firm and springy to the touch.

4. When cool, split the cake into two halves and sandwich together with the prepared Vanilla Custard Filling.

5. Spread some pure maple syrup over the top of the cake and sprinkle with desiccated coconut. Complete by decorating with a small fresh flower, placed in the centre of the cake.

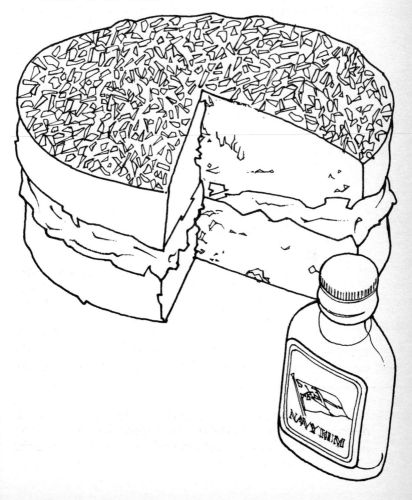

CAROB ORANGE CAKE

Serves 6

Rich in flavour and colour, this sandwich cake makes an attractive sight on a tea-time table.

Imperial (Metric)	American
6 oz (170g) polyunsaturated margarine	¾ cupful polyunsaturated margarine
4 oz (115g) raw cane sugar	⅔ cupful raw cane sugar
Finely grated zest of 1 orange	Finely grated zest of 1 orange
3 eggs, lightly beaten	3 eggs, lightly beaten
6 oz (170g) wholemeal flour	1¼ cupsful wholewheat flour
1 oz (30g) carob powder	¼ cupful carob powder
2 teaspoonsful baking powder	2 teaspoonsful baking powder

Filling and Decoration:	*Filling and Decoration:*
Orange Custard Filling (page 178)	Orange Custard Filling (page 178)
2 orange slices	2 orange slices

1. Cream the margarine, sugar and grated orange zest together until pale and fluffy.

2. Gradually incorporate the beaten eggs, adding a little at a time and beating well after each addition.

3. Fold in the flour, carob powder and baking powder.

4. Divide the mixture between two 7 inch (18cm) round cake tins and bake at 375°F/190°C (Gas Mark 5) for 25-30 minutes, until nicely risen and firm to the touch.

5. Prepare the Orange Custard Filling as indicated and spread a thin layer of the custard over the top of one of the cakes. Use the remaining orange custard to sandwich the two cakes together.

6. Cut the orange slices into quarter segments and use these to decorate the top of the cake.

CAROB COATED WALNUT LOAF CAKE

Makes one 2 lb (900g) loaf cake

Imperial (Metric)
1 lb (455g) wholemeal flour
3 teaspoonsful baking powder
4 oz (115g) light Muscovado
  sugar
4 oz (115g) walnuts, chopped
2 eggs, lightly beaten
2 oz (55g) polyunsaturated
  margarine, melted and
  cooled
½ pint (285ml) milk

Coating and Decoration:
Plain Carob Coating (page 183)
10 walnut halves

American
4 cupsful wholewheat flour
3 teaspoonsful baking powder
⅔ cupful light Muscovado
  sugar
¾ cupful walnuts, chopped
2 eggs, lightly beaten
¼ cupful polyunsaturated
  margarine, melted and
  cooled
1⅓ cupsful milk

Coating and Decoration:
Plain Carob Coating (page 183)
10 walnut halves

1. Place the flour, baking powder, sugar and walnuts in a mixing bowl, combining them well.

2. Make a well in the centre of the dry ingredients and pour in the beaten eggs, melted margarine and milk, blending well to give a soft dropping consistency.

3. Spoon the mixture into a greased 2 lb (900g) loaf tin, smoothing over the top, then bake at 350°F/180°C (Gas Mark 4) for 1¼-1½ hours, until nicely risen and firm to the touch. Test the cake by inserting a fine skewer into it; if the skewer comes out clean, the cake is cooked through.

4. Allow the cake to cool thoroughly, then spread the carob coating on top, allowing some of it to drizzle down the sides of the cake. Complete by decorating with some walnut halves. Leave the Carob Coating to set before serving.

CAROB COCONUT CAKE

Serves 6-8

A carob, vanilla and orange flavoured cake, coated with pure maple syrup and masked in coconut.

Imperial (Metric)	American
4 eggs, separated	4 eggs, separated
4 oz (115g) Vanilla Sugar (page 189)	⅔ cupful Vanilla Sugar (page 189)
Finely grated zest of 1 orange	Finely grated zest of 1 orange
3½ oz (100g) wholemeal flour	¾ cupful + 1 tablespoonful wholewheat flour
¾ oz (20g) carob powder	2 tablespoonsful carob powder

Coating and Decoration:	*Coating and Decoration:*
4-5 tablespoonsful pure maple syrup	4-5 tablespoonsful pure maple syrup
2 oz (55g) desiccated coconut	⅔ cupful desiccated coconut
Fresh flower	Fresh flower

1. Place the egg yolks, Vanilla Sugar and grated orange zest in a mixing bowl and whisk until the mixture lightens and becomes thick and creamy.

2. Mix the flour and carob powder together, combining them well.

3. In a separate bowl, whisk the egg whites until they stand in stiff peaks. Now carefully fold the whisked egg whites into the egg yolk mixture, incorporating alternately with the dry ingredients, beginning and ending with the whisked egg whites. Fold in the ingredients as lightly as possible, so that the whites retain as much of their volume as possible, resulting in a meltingly light cake.

4. Pour the mixture into a greased 8 inch (20cm) round,

deep cake tin, then bake at 375°F/190°C (Gas Mark 5) for 30-35 minutes, until nicely risen and firm to the touch.

5. Allow the cake to cool thoroughly, then using a pastry brush, coat the sides of the cake completely with pure maple syrup, then roll in desiccated coconut. Now coat the top of the cake with maple syrup and cover completely with the desiccated coconut. Complete the cake by decorating with a brightly coloured fresh flower, preferably of an exotic appearance.

CAROB COATED LEMON CAKE

Flavoured with lemon zest and almonds, this light-as-a-feather wholemeal sponge cake is topped with a melted carob coating.

Imperial (Metric)	American
4 eggs, separated	4 eggs, separated
4 oz (115 g) raw cane sugar	⅔ cupful raw cane sugar
Finely grated zest of 1 lemon	Finely grated zest of 1 lemon
3 oz (85 g) wholemeal flour	¾ cupful wholewheat flour
1½ oz (45 g) ground almonds	½ cupful ground almonds

Coating and Decoration:
Plain Carob Coating (page 183)
12 split blanched almonds
Small yellow or white fresh flower

Coating and Decoration:
Plain Carob Coating (page 183)
12 split blanched almonds
Small yellow or white fresh flower

1. Whisk the egg yolks, sugar and finely grated lemon zest together until the mixture lightens and becomes thick and creamy.

2. Mix the flour and ground almonds together, combining them well.

3. In a separate bowl, whisk the egg whites until they stand in stiff peaks, then carefully fold into the creamed egg yolk mixture, adding alternately with the dry ingredients, and beginning and ending with the whisked egg whites. Incorporate the ingredients as carefully and as lightly as possible, so that the whites retain as much of their volume as possible, resulting in a feathery light cake.

4. Pour the mixture into a greased 8 inch (20 cm) round, deep cake tin and bake at 375°F/190°C (Gas Mark 5) for 35-40 minutes, or until the cake is well risen and firm to the touch.

5. Allow the lemon cake to cool thoroughly, then spread the Carob Coating on top, allowing some of it to drizzle down the sides of the cake. Place some split blanched almonds on top of the Carob Coating to decorate, and complete the decoration with a small yellow or white fresh flower, placed in the centre of the cake.

CAROB AND ALMOND LAYER CAKE

Serves 6-8

Three layers of carob and almond flavoured sponge are
sandwiched together with toasted flaked almonds and an
orange custard filling.

Imperial (Metric)	American
4 eggs	4 eggs
3 oz (85 g) raw cane sugar	½ cupful raw cane sugar
1 oz (30 g) Vanilla Sugar (page 189)	2 tablespoonsful Vanilla Sugar (page 189)
3 oz (85 g) wholemeal flour	¾ cupful wholewheat flour
¾ oz (20 g) carob powder	2 tablespoonsful carob powder
¾ oz (20 g) ground almonds	2 tablespoonsful ground almonds
¾ oz (20 g) polyunsaturated margarine, melted and cooled	2 tablespoonsful polyunsaturated margarine, melted and cooled

Filling and Decoration:	*Filling and Decoration:*
Orange Custard Filling (page 178)	Orange Custard Filling (page 178)
4 oz (115 g) flaked almonds, lightly toasted	1 cupful slivered almonds, lightly toasted
Quartered orange slices	Quartered orange slices

1. Place the eggs, raw cane sugar and Vanilla Sugar in a
   mixing bowl and whisk until thick, creamy and tripled
   in volume. (The whisk should leave a distinct trail when
   lifted from the mixture.)

2. Mix the flour, carob powder and ground almonds
   together, combining them well, then carefully fold
   into the egg mixture, adding alternately with the
   melted margarine. Incorporate the ingredients as lightly
   and as carefully as possible, so that the mixture retains
   as much of its volume as possible.

3. Pour the mixture into a Swiss roll tin measuring approximately 9 x 13 inches (23 x 33 cm), lined with greased greaseproof paper. Spread the mixture evenly with a palette knife, then bake at 400°F/200°C (Gas Mark 6) for about 12 minutes, until the cake is firm and springy to the touch.

4. When cool, turn the cake out of the tin and peel off the lining paper. Trim the crusty edges off the sponge and cut crossways into three equally sized rectangles.

5. Prepare the Orange Custard Filling by the indicated method and spread a thin coating of the filling over the top layer of the cake.

6. Reserve about ½ oz (15 g) of the toasted almonds for decoration, then fold the remainder into the Orange Custard filling. Sandwich the three cake layers together with this filling.

7. Decorate the cake with some quartered orange slices and complete by sprinkling with the reserved toasted flaked almonds.

CAROB AND SULTANA LOAF CAKE

Makes one 1 lb (455g) loaf cake

A tasty loaf cake, flavoured with vanilla and orange and topped with a contrasting orange-flavoured butter cream.

Imperial (Metric)	American
7 oz (200g) wholemeal flour	1¾ cupsful wholewheat flour
1 teaspoonful bicarbonate of soda	1 teaspoonful bicarbonate of soda
1 teaspoonful cream of tartar	1 teaspoonful cream of tartar
1 oz (30g) carob powder	¼ cupful carob powder
1 oz (30g) ground almonds	¼ cupful ground almonds
2 oz (55g) Vanilla Sugar (page 189)	⅓ cupful Vanilla Sugar (page 189)
Finely grated zest of 1 orange	Finely grated zest of 1 orange
4 oz (115g) sultanas	⅔ cupful golden seedless raisins
3 oz (85g) polyunsaturated margarine	⅓ cupful polyunsaturated margarine
1 tablespoonful clear honey	1 tablespoonful clear honey
2 eggs, lightly beaten	2 eggs, lightly beaten
3 tablespoonsful natural yogurt	3 tablespoonsful natural yogurt

Topping:	*Topping:*
Orange Butter Cream (page 182)	Orange Butter Cream (page 182)
Quartered orange slices	Quartered orange slices

1. Place the flour, bicarbonate of soda, cream of tartar, carob powder and ground almonds in a mixing bowl, combining them well.

2. Fold in the Vanilla Sugar, finely grated orange zest and sultanas.

3. Melt the margarine and honey together in a saucepan set over a moderate heat, without allowing to boil.

4. Make a well in the centre of the dry ingredients and pour in the melted margarine and honey, and beaten eggs. Draw the flour over the well and begin mixing the ingredients together, then add sufficient natural yogurt to give a soft dropping consistency.

5. Spoon the mixture into a greased 1 lb (455 g) loaf tin, smoothing over the top, and bake at 350°F/180°C (Gas Mark 4) for 50-60 minutes, until firm to the touch. (Test by inserting a skewer into the cake; if the skewer comes out clean, the cake is cooked through.)

6. Allow the loaf cake to cool thoroughly, then spread the Orange Butter Cream on top. Complete the cake by decorating with some quartered orange slices.

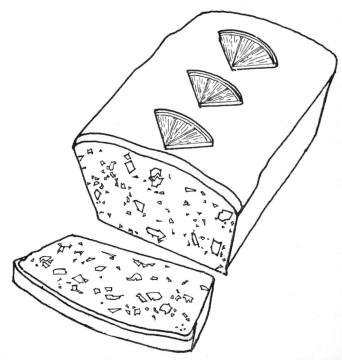

CAROB AND APRICOT TEABREAD

Makes one 1 lb (455g) loaf cake

Imperial (Metric)
6 oz (170g) wholemeal flour
1 oz (30g) ground almonds
2 teaspoonsful baking powder
4 oz (115g) polyunsaturated
  margarine
1 oz (30g) carob powder
4 oz (115g) dried apricots,
  diced
2 oz (55g) nibbed almonds
2 tablespoonsful clear honey
3-4 tablespoonsful natural
  yogurt or milk
8-10 whole blanched almonds

American
1½ cupsful wholewheat flour
¼ cupful ground almonds
2 teaspoonsful baking powder
½ cupful polyunsaturated
  margarine
¼ cupful carob powder
⅔ cupful dried apricots, diced
½ cupful nibbed almonds
2 tablespoonsful clear honey
3-4 tablespoonsful natural
  yogurt or milk
8-10 whole blanched almonds

1. Place the flour, ground almonds and baking powder in a mixing bowl, combining them well.

2. Rub the margarine into the dry ingredients, until a breadcrumb consistency is obtained.

3. Fold in the carob powder, dried apricots and nibbed almonds.

4. Make a well in the centre of the ingredients and pour in the honey. Begin binding the ingredients together, incorporating a sufficient amount of natural yogurt or milk to give a soft dropping consistency.

5. Spoon the mixture into a greased 1 lb (455g) loaf tin, spreading evenly, then dot the surface of the cake mixture with some whole blanched almonds.

6. Bake at 350°F/180°C (Gas Mark 4) for about 1 hour, until nicely risen and firm to the touch. Test the cake

by inserting a fine skewer into it; if the skewer comes out clean, the cake is cooked through.

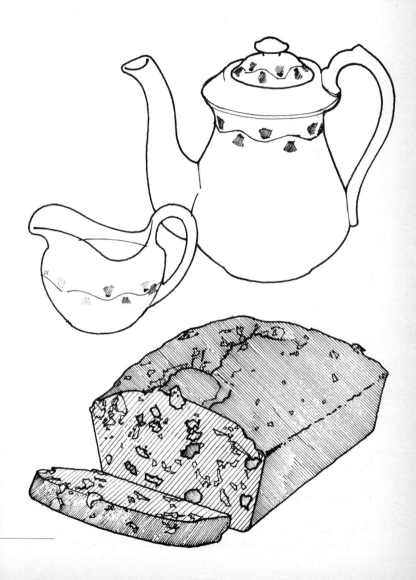

MARBLED CAKE

Makes one 8 inch (20cm) cake

Intermingling layers of plain and carob-flavoured sponge are contained in this wholemeal cake.

Imperial (Metric)
6 oz (170g) polyunsaturated margarine
5 oz (140g) light Muscovado sugar
3 eggs, lightly beaten
5 oz (140g) wholemeal flour
2½ teaspoonsful baking powder
1 oz (30g) carob powder
1 tablespoonful natural yogurt or milk

Coating and Decoration:
Plain Carob Coating (page 183)
Split blanched almonds, lightly toasted

American
¾ cupful polyunsaturated margarine
⅔ cupful + 2 tablespoonsful light Muscovado sugar
3 eggs, lightly beaten
1¼ cupsful wholewheat flour
2½ teaspoonsful baking powder
¼ cupful carob powder
1 tablespoonful natural yogurt or milk

Coating and Decoration:
Plain Carob Coating (page 183)
Split blanched almonds, lightly toasted

1. Cream the margarine and Muscovado sugar together until light and fluffy.

2. Gradually incorporate the beaten eggs, adding a little at a time and beating well after each addition.

3. Fold in the flour and baking powder, then transfer half the quantity of the cake mixture to a separate bowl. Now fold the carob powder and yogurt or milk into one of the halved quantities, leaving the remaining half plain.

4. Place alternate tablespoonsful of the two mixtures into a greased 8 inch (20cm) round cake tin, so that the

plain and carob-flavoured sponge mixtures intermingle in the cake. Lightly smooth over the top, then bake at 350°F/180°C (Gas Mark 4) for 40-45 minutes, until nicely risen and firm to the touch.

5. Allow the marbled cake to cool, then spread the Carob Coating evenly on top, allowing some of it to drizzle down the sides of the cake. Complete by decorating with some toasted almonds.

CAROB AND ORANGE BUN CAKES

Makes 10-12

Imperial (Metric)	American
2 oz (55g) polyunsaturated margarine	¼ cupful polyunsaturated margarine
2 oz (55g) Vanilla Sugar (page 189)	⅓ cupful Vanilla Sugar (page 189)
Finely grated zest of 1 orange	Finely grated zest of 1 orange
1 egg, lightly beaten	1 egg, lightly beaten
3½ oz (100g) wholemeal flour	¾ cupful + 1 tablespoonful wholewheat flour
½ oz (15g) carob powder	1 tablespoonful carob powder
1 teaspoonful baking powder	1 teaspoonful baking powder
Strained juice of 1 small orange	Strained juice of 1 small orange

Coating and Decoration:
Plain Carob Coating (page 183)
Split blanched almonds,
   lightly toasted

Coating and Decoration:
Plain Carob Coating (page 183)
Split blanched almonds,
   lightly toasted

1. Cream the margarine, Vanilla Sugar and orange zest together until light and fluffy.

2. Gradually incorporate the beaten egg, adding a little at a time, then fold in the flour, carob powder and baking powder, together with sufficient orange juice to give a soft dropping consistency.

3. Spoon the mixture into well-greased, deep bun tins and bake at 350°F/180°C (Gas Mark 4) for 12-15 minutes, until nicely risen and firm to the touch.

4. Turn the bun cakes out of the tins and allow to cool thoroughly, then spread with the Carob Coating. Complete the cakes by decorating with some lightly toasted almonds.

2.

SPECIAL OCCASION GÂTEAUX AND DESSERTS

When planning a natural-food meal for a special occasion or dinner party, the most difficult choice is quite often what to serve for dessert.

The gâteaux and desserts that I have included in this section will, I think, please the most discerning of dinner party guests and in many cases your guests will be astonished to learn that they are made with natural ingredients. As wholefoods grow in popularity, moreover, natural-food dinner parties are becoming increasingly acceptable and are often greatly appreciated by the guests, particularly when they discover, as in the case of carob, that they can eat a natural chocolate substitute without feeling those familiar pangs of guilt.

CARIBBEAN PINEAPPLE AND COCONUT GÂTEAU

Serves 8-10

The flavour of this tempting gâteau is hard to resist – it comprises a meltingly light carob cake flavoured with vanilla and almonds, sandwiched together with a vanilla custard filling and natural dried pineapple. The gâteau is then coated with pure maple syrup and sprinkled with freshly grated coconut.

Imperial (Metric)
6 eggs, separated
4 oz (115g) Vanilla Sugar
  (page 189)
3 oz (85g) wholemeal flour
1 oz (30g) ground almonds
¾ oz (20g) carob powder

Filling:
Vanilla Cream Filling
  (page 177)
1 extra egg white, stiffly beaten
4 oz (115g) dried pineapple,
  chopped

Coating and Decoration:
1-2 tablespoonsful pure
  maple syrup
Freshly grated or desiccated
  coconut
Small flower or flower petals

American
6 eggs, separated
⅔ cupful Vanilla Sugar
  (page 189)
¾ cupful wholewheat flour
¼ cupful ground almonds
2 tablespoonsful carob powder

Filling:
Vanilla Cream Filling
  (page 177)
1 extra egg white, stiffly beaten
1 cupful dried pineapple,
  chopped

Coating and Decoration:
1-2 tablespoonsful pure
  maple syrup
Freshly grated or desiccated
  coconut
Small flower or flower petals

1. Place the egg yolks and Vanilla Sugar in a mixing bowl and whisk well until the mixture lightens and becomes thick and creamy.

2. Mix the flour, ground almonds and carob powder together, combining them well.

3. In a separate bowl, whisk the egg whites until they stand in stiff peaks. Now carefully fold the whisked egg whites and dry ingredients into the egg yolk mixture, incorporating them alternately, and beginning and ending with the egg whites. Fold in the ingredients lightly so that the whites retain as much of their volume as possible, resulting in a meltingly light cake.

4. Pour the mixture into a greased 9 inch(23 cm) round, deep cake tin and bake at 375°F/190°C (Gas Mark 5) for 35-40 minutes, until nicely risen and firm to the touch.

5. Prepare the Vanilla Custard Filling by the indicated method, incorporating three stiffly beaten egg whites rather than the normal two. After incorporating the egg whites, fold the dried pineapple into the Vanilla Custard.

6. When cool, split the carob cake into two halves and sandwich together with the Vanilla Custard and Pineapple Filling.

7. Coat the top of the gâteau with pure maple syrup and sprinkle with freshly grated (or desiccated) coconut. Complete the gâteau by decorating with a brightly coloured flower or flower petals.

CAROB COATED ALMOND CHOUX RING

Serves 6-8

If your family has a passion for éclairs, they will love this carob-coated choux pastry ring. Made with wholemeal flour, choux pastry gives unexpectedly delicious results – it is light and fluffy yet has the delicious nutty flavour and chewy texture characteristic of wholemeal baking. Here the choux pastry ring encases a vanilla custard and toasted almond filling and is topped with a dark and delicious carob coating.

Imperial (Metric)	American
Wholemeal Choux Pastry:	*Wholemeal Choux Pastry:*
2 oz (55g) polyunsaturated margarine	¼ cupful polyunsaturated margarine
¼ pint (140ml) water	⅔ cupful water
2½ oz (70g) wholemeal flour	⅔ cupful wholewheat flour
Pinch of sea salt	Pinch of sea salt
2 eggs	2 eggs
Filling and Coating:	*Filling and Coating:*
Vanilla Cream Filling (page 177)	Vanilla Custard Filling (page 177)
3 oz (85g) flaked almonds, lightly toasted	¾ cupful slivered almonds, lightly toasted
Plain Carob Coating (page 183)	Plain Carob Coating (page 183)

1. To make the choux pastry, place the margarine and water in a saucepan and bring to the boil, stirring all the time until the margarine has melted.

2. When boiling point is reached, remove from the heat and add the flour and sea salt all at once. Beat vigorously with a wooden spoon until thoroughly blended, then return the saucepan to a moderate heat and continue beating until the paste forms a coherent mass and leaves the sides of the saucepan clean. Now remove

from the heat and beat in the eggs, adding one at a time, until the paste is smooth and glossy.

3. Place the choux pastry in a piping bag fitted with a large plain nozzle, then pipe an 8 inch (20cm) ring onto a lightly greased baking sheet.

4. Bake the ring at 425°F/220°C (Gas Mark 7) for 15 minutes, then reduce the oven temperature to 375°F/190°C (Gas Mark 5) and bake for a further 10-15 minutes, until the pastry is golden brown and crusty to the touch. Now switch off the oven, make a few slits in the ring to allow the steam to escape, then leave to dry out in the switched-off oven, with the door ajar, for about 10 minutes.

5. Prepare the Vanilla Custard Filling by the indicated method, then fold in the lightly toasted almonds.

6. Carefully split the choux ring in half and sandwich together with the toasted almond and Vanilla Custard Filling. Spread the Carob Coating over the ring and leave to set before serving.

PROFITEROLES

Serves 6-8

Wholemeal Choux Pastry (See method given for Almond
  Choux Ring page 60)
Vanilla Custard Filling (page 177)
Plain Carob Coating (page 183)
  or
Carob and Vanilla Cream Sauce (page 184)

1. Prepare a quantity of wholemeal choux pastry, using
   the same method as that given for the Almond Choux
   Ring.

2. Spoon the choux pastry into a piping bag fitted with a
   large plain nozzle, then pipe small balls of pastry onto
   greased baking sheets.

3. Bake the choux pastry balls at 425°F/220°C (Gas Mark
   7) for 10 minutes, then reduce the oven temperature to
   375°F/190°C (Gas Mark 5) and bake for a further 12-15
   minutes, until golden brown and crusty to the touch.
   Now switch off the oven, make slits in the choux
   pastry balls to enable the steam to escape, then leave to
   dry out in the switched-off oven, with the door ajar, for
   about 10 minutes.

4. When cool, fill the choux pastry balls with the Vanilla
   Custard Filling, then pile onto a serving dish, in
   pyramid form.

5. Serve the profiteroles either topped with a Plain Carob
   Coating, allowed to set and served cold, or topped with
   a warm Carob and Vanilla Cream Sauce, poured over
   the profiteroles at the time of serving.

JAMAICAN CREAM MOUSSE

Serves 4

Imperial (Metric)	American
1 x 2½oz (75g) carob bar	1 x 2½oz carob bar
1 tablespoonful dark Jamaican rum or *Tia Maria*	1 tablespoonful dark Jamaican rum or *Tia Maria*
3 eggs, separated	3 eggs, separated
¼ pint (140ml) double cream	⅔ cupful heavy cream
Decoration:	*Decoration:*
½oz (7g) flaked almonds, lightly toasted	1 tablespoonful slivered almonds, lightly toasted

1. Break the carob bar into small pieces and place in a heat-resistant bowl. Set the bowl over a saucepan of gently simmering water until the carob is fully melted, then blend in the rum or *Tia Maria*.

2. Remove from the heat and stir the egg yolks into the melted carob, adding one at a time and beating well after each addition.

3. Whip the cream until it stands in firm peaks and reserve one tablespoonful for decoration. Fold the remaining cream into the carob and egg mixture.

4. Whisk the egg whites until they stand in stiff peaks, then carefully fold into the mixture, making sure that the whites retain as much of their volume as possible, so that the finished mousse is meltingly light.

5. Pour the mixture into individual serving glasses and leave to set in the refrigerator for 2-3 hours.

6. Shortly before serving, pipe the reserved whipped cream onto the desserts, dotting with some lightly toasted flaked almonds.

ICED JAMAICAN CREAM MOUSSE

Prepare the carob mousse mixture by the method on page 63. Pour into individual serving glasses and freeze until firm. Allow the iced mousse to soften slightly in the refrigerator before serving, garnishing with some brightly coloured fresh flowers.

CAROB COATED RASPBERRY ROULADE

Serves 6

A melted carob coating covers this wholemeal, orange-flavoured roll, with its raspberry and cream filling.

Imperial (Metric)	American
4 eggs	4 eggs
4 oz (115g) raw cane sugar	⅔ cupful raw cane sugar
Finely grated zest of 1 orange	Finely grated zest of 1 orange
4 oz (115g) wholemeal flour	1 cupful wholewheat flour
¾ oz (20g) polyunsaturated margarine, melted and cooled	2 tablespoonsful polyunsaturated margarine, melted and cooled

Filling and Decoration:	*Filling and Decoration:*
8 oz (225g) raspberries	2 cupsful raspberries
Light Muscovado sugar	Light Muscovado sugar
¼ pint (140ml) double cream	⅔ cupful heavy cream
Fresh raspberry or other leaves	Fresh raspberry or other leaves
Plain Carob Coating (page 183)	Plain Carob Coating (page 183)

1. Whisk the eggs, sugar and finely grated orange zest together until thick, creamy and tripled in volume. (The whisk should leave a distinct trail when lifted from the mixture.)

2. Carefully fold in the flour, adding alternately with the melted margarine. Incorporate the flour as quickly and

as lightly as possible, so that the mixture retains as much of its volume as possible.

3. Pour the mixture into a Swiss roll tin measuring approximately 9 x 13 inches (23 x 33 cm), and lined with greased greaseproof paper. Spread the mixture evenly with a palette knife, then bake at 400°F/200°C (Gas Mark 6) for about 12 minutes, until golden brown and springy to the touch.

4. Lay a piece of greaseproof paper on a flat surface. Turn the sponge onto the greaseproof paper and peel off the lining paper. Trim the crusty edges off the sponge, then lay a second piece of greaseproof paper on top. Carefully roll up the sponge, with the greaseproof paper inside.

5. Meanwhile, prepare the filling. First hull and rinse the raspberries and drain very thoroughly. Reserve about 6 raspberries for decoration, then sprinkle the remainder with a little Muscovado sugar and set aside to allow the sugar to soak in.

6. Whip the cream until it stands in stiff peaks, then fold the raspberries into the cream. Unroll the sponge, discarding the greaseproof paper, then cover with the raspberry and cream filling and carefully re-roll.

7. Spread the Carob Coating all over the surface of the roll, spreading evenly. Complete by decorating with the reserved raspberries and some fresh raspberry, or other, leaves.

MOCHA GÂTEAU

Serves 6-8

Carob and decaffeinated coffee are combined to make a mocha-flavoured cake, encasing a creamy vanilla custard filling.

Imperial (Metric)

Mocha Syrup:
1 tablespoonful carob powder
1 tablespoonful decaffeinated coffee
2 fl oz (60 ml) boiling water

Cake:
4 eggs
4 oz (115 g) light Muscovado sugar
4 oz (115 g) wholemeal flour

Filling and Decoration:
Vanilla Custard Filling (page 177)
2 tablespoonsful stiffly whipped double cream
Small flowers

American

Mocha Syrup:
1 tablespoonful carob powder
1 tablespoonful decaffeinated coffee
¼ cupful boiling water

Cake:
4 eggs
⅔ cupful light Muscovado sugar
1 cupful wholewheat flour

Filling and Decoration:
Vanilla Custard Filling (page 177)
2 tablespoonsful stiffly whipped heavy cream
Small flowers

1. First prepare the mocha syrup. To do this, place the carob powder and decaffeinated coffee in a small bowl and add the boiling water, blending until smooth and glossy.

2. To prepare the cake, whisk the eggs and Muscovado sugar together until pale, creamy and tripled in volume. (The whisk should leave a distinct trail when lifted from the mixture.) When the mixture reaches this consistency, pour in the prepared mocha syrup and continue whisking until thoroughly blended.

3. Now carefully fold in the flour, working as lightly as possible so that the mixture retains as much of its volume as possible.

4. Pour into a Swiss roll tin measuring 9 x 13 inches (23 x 33cm) and lined with greased greaseproof paper. Spread the mixture evenly with a palette knife and bake at 400°F/200°C (Gas Mark 6) for about 12 minutes, until firm and springy to the touch.

5. When cool, turn the mocha sponge out of the tin and peel off the lining paper. Trim the crusty edges off the cake, then cut crossways into three equally sized rectangles.

6. Prepare the Vanilla Custard Filling by the indicated method, then use to sandwich the three mocha rectangles together. If desired, pipe a little whipped cream on top of the gâteau and complete by decorating with some small fresh flowers.

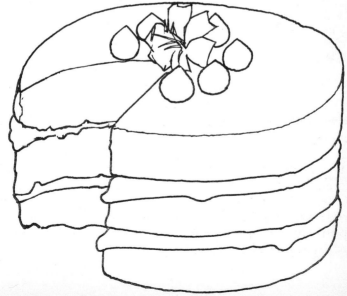

CAROB HAZELNUT MERINGUE GÂTEAU

Serves 8

This carob-flavoured meringue gâteau is dotted with
toasted hazelnuts and sandwiched together with a vanilla
custard filling.

Imperial (Metric)	American
6 egg whites	6 egg whites
10 oz (285 g) light Muscovado sugar	1⅔ cupful light Muscovado sugar
1 oz (30 g) carob powder	¼ cupful carob powder
8 oz (225 g) hazelnuts, finely chopped and lightly toasted	1½ cupful hazelnuts, finely chopped and lightly toasted

Filling and Decoration:	*Filling and Decoration:*
Vanilla Custard Filling (page 177)	Vanilla Custard Filling (page 177)
Fresh flower	Fresh flower
6 whole roasted hazelnuts	6 whole roasted hazelnuts
Clear honey	Clear honey

1. Draw three 7 inch (18 cm) diameter circles on greaseproof paper. Grease the circles well and place on
   baking sheets.

2. To make the meringue, whisk the egg whites until they
   stand in stiff peaks. Add half the quantity of sugar and
   the carob powder, then continue whisking until the
   whites regain their former stiffness. Now carefully fold
   in the remaining sugar and the toasted hazelnuts.

3. Spoon the mixture evenly onto the three marked
   circles, then bake at 250°F/130°C (Gas Mark ½) for 2-3
   hours, until the meringue is crisp and dry.

4. Meanwhile, prepare the Vanilla Custard Filling by the indicated method. Carefully remove the lining paper from the meringue circles, then sandwich together with the Vanilla Custard Filling.

5. Complete the gâteau by decorating with a brightly coloured fresh flower, placed in the centre of the gâteau surrounded by a circle of whole hazelnuts, secured with a little clear honey.

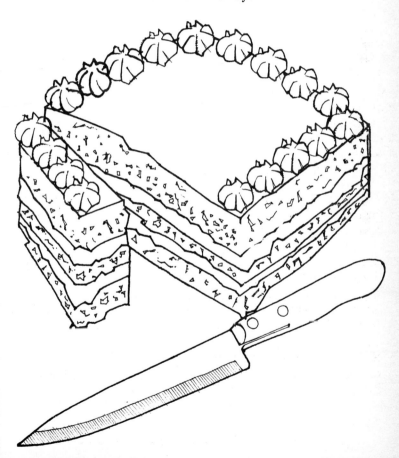

TROPICAL FRUIT GÂTEAU

Serves 8-10

Laden with kiwi fruit, pineapple and mango, with an exotic-flavoured orange and passion fruit filling, for a true taste of the tropics.

Imperial (Metric)	**American**
6 eggs, separated	6 eggs, separated
4 oz (115 g) light Muscovado sugar	⅔ cupful light Muscovado sugar
Finely grated zest of 1 orange	Finely grated zest of 1 orange
3 oz (85 g) wholemeal flour	¾ cupful wholewheat flour
1 oz (30 g) ground almonds	¼ cupful ground almonds
¾ oz (20 g) carob powder	2 tablespoonsful carob powder
Filling and Decoration:	*Filling and Decoration:*
Orange and Passion Fruit Custard Filling (page 180)	Orange and Passion Fruit Custard Filling (page 180)
1 small pineapple, with a good tuft of leaves	1 small pineapple, with a good tuft of leaves
1 small papaya	1 small papaya
4 kiwi fruit	4 kiwi fruit
Pure maple syrup	Pure maple syrup

1. Place the egg yolks, Muscovado sugar and grated orange zest in a mixing bowl and whisk well until the mixture lightens and becomes thick and creamy.

2. Mix the flour, ground almonds and carob powder together.

3. In a separate bowl, whisk the egg whites until they stand in stiff peaks, then carefully fold into the egg yolk mixture, adding alternately with the dry ingredients, and beginning and ending with the whisked egg whites. Incorporate the ingredients as lightly as possible, so that the whites retain as much of their volume as possible, resulting in a feathery light cake.

4. Pour the mixture into a greased 9 inch (23cm) round, deep cake tin, then bake at 375°F/190°C (Gas Mark 5) for 35-40 minutes, until well risen and firm to the touch.

5. Meanwhile, prepare the Orange and Passion Fruit Custard Filling by the indicated method.

6. To prepare the fruit, slice the top and base off the pineapple, then cut into rings, removing the outer peel, small brown 'eyes' and hard centre core. Dice the pineapple flesh into small chunks. Trim the tuft of leaves, discarding any withered parts, and reserve for decoration.

7. Peel and seed the papaya, then dice half the fruit into small chunks. Cut the remaining half into long segments. Peel the kiwi fruit and dice one of the fruit into small chunks; cut the remaining kiwi fruit into round slices.

8. Slice the carob cake into two halves, then spread a thin layer of the Orange and Passion Fruit Filling over the top half.

9. Fold the diced pineapple, diced papaya and diced kiwi fruit into the remaining custard filling, then use this filling to sandwich the carob cake together.

10. To decorate the top of the gâteau, first place the trimmed tuft of pineapple leaves in the centre of the cake. Place the papaya segments in a ring around the outer edge of the cake. Now arrange the kiwi fruit slices on top of the gâteau, filling the space between the tuft of pineapple leaves and the ring of papaya segments.

11. Brush the fruit on top of the gâteau with some pure maple syrup, to add a glossy finish.

CAROB POTS DE CRÈME

Serves 6

Small pots of carob, vanilla and rum flavoured custard.

Imperial (Metric)	American
¾ pint (425 ml) milk	2 cupsful milk
1 vanilla pod, split lengthways	1 vanilla bean, split lengthways
2 x 2½ oz (75g) carob bars	2 x 2½ ounces carob bars
1 tablespoonful dark rum	1 tablespoonful dark rum
1 oz (30g) light Muscovado sugar	2 tablespoonsful light Muscovado sugar
4 egg yolks	4 egg yolks

Decoration:	*Decoration:*
¼ pint double cream, chilled and stiffly whipped for piping	⅔ cupful heavy cream, chilled and stiffly whipped for piping
Grated block carob	Grated block carob

1. Scald the vanilla pod in the milk, then cover and set aside to infuse for about 15 minutes, so that the flavour of the vanilla pod penetrates the milk. Remove the vanilla pod after the infusion time, then re-heat the milk to simmering point.

2. Meanwhile, break the carob bars into pieces and place in a heat-resistant bowl. Set the bowl over a saucepan of gently simmering water, to melt the carob. When melted, add the dark rum and Muscovado sugar, blending well.

3. Away from the heat, blend the egg yolks into the melted carob mixture, incorporating one at a time and mixing well after each addition.

4. Now slowly pour the hot, vanilla-flavoured milk onto the carob mixture in a thin stream, stirring continuously and blending very thoroughly.

5. Strain the mixture into petits pots or individual ramekin dishes and cook *au bain-marie* by standing in a roasting tin or ovenproof dish containing sufficient boiling water to cover two-thirds of the depth of the small pots.

6. Cook the custards at 325°F/170°C (Gas Mark 3) for 30-35 minutes, or until set. Test the custards by inserting a fine skewer into them; if the skewer comes out clean, the custards are cooked.

7. Allow the custards to cool slightly after removing from the oven, then chill very thoroughly in the refrigerator.

8. Shortly before serving, decorate the custards with some decoratively piped whipped cream, sprinkled with some grated block carob.

CAROB AND ORANGE ROULADE

Serves 6

Flavoured with carob and orange, this melt-in-the-mouth sponge roll is perfect for a special occasion.

Imperial (Metric)
4 eggs
4 oz (115 g) light Muscovado sugar
Finely grated zest of 1 orange
3½ oz (100 g) wholemeal flour
¾ oz (20 g) carob powder
1 tablespoonful freshly-squeezed orange juice
½ oz (15 g) polyunsaturated margarine, melted and cooled

Filling and Decoration:
½ pint (285 ml) double cream, chilled and stiffly whipped for piping
Small fresh flowers

American
4 eggs
⅔ cupful light Muscovado sugar
Finely grated zest of 1 orange
¾ cupful + 1 tablespoonful wholewheat flour
2 tablespoonsful carob powder
1 tablespoonful freshly squeezed orange juice
1 tablespoonful polyunsaturated margarine, melted and cooled

Filling and Decoration:
1⅓ cupsful heavy cream, chilled and stiffly whipped for piping
Small fresh flowers

1. Whisk the eggs, Muscovado sugar and finely grated orange zest together until thick, creamy and tripled in volume. (The whisk should leave a distinct trail when lifted from the mixture.)

2. Carefully fold the flour and carob powder into the egg mixture, incorporating alternately with the fresh orange juice and melted margarine. Fold in the dry ingredients as quickly and as lightly as possible, so that the mixture retains as much of its volume as possible, resulting in a deliciously light cake.

3. Pour the mixture into a Swiss roll tin measuring approximately 9 x 13 inches (23 x 33cm), and lined with greased greaseproof paper. Spread the mixture evenly with a palette knife, then bake at 400°F/200°C (Gas Mark 6) for about 12 minutes, until firm and springy to the touch.

4. Lay a large piece of greaseproof paper on a flat surface. Turn the sponge out onto the greaseproof paper and peel off the lining paper. Now trim the crusty edges off the sponge, then lay a second piece of greaseproof paper on top. Carefully roll up the sponge, with the greaseproof paper inside.

5. When the sponge has cooled, unroll and discard the greaseproof paper. Reserve about 2 tablespoonsful of the whipped cream for decoration, then spread the remainder over the sponge and re-roll.

6. Use the reserved whipped cream to pipe a line of rosettes on top of the roulade, interspacing with some brightly-coloured fresh flowers. Place several fresh flowers at each side of the roulade, around the base, to complete the decoration.

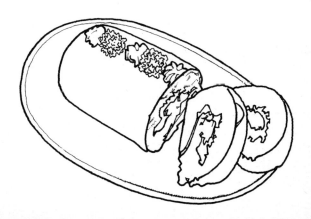

PEAR AND VANILLA GÂTEAU

Serves 8-10

A flavour-rich, all-year-round gâteau, covered with vanilla-poached pears, almonds and kiwi fruit, and sandwiched together with a pear and vanilla custard filling.

Imperial (Metric)	American
Carob Cake:	*Carob Cake:*
6 eggs, separated	6 eggs, separated
4 oz (115 g) Vanilla Sugar (page 189)	⅔ cupful Vanilla Sugar (page 189)
3½ oz (100 g) wholemeal flour	¾ cupful + tablespoonful wholewheat flour
½ oz (15 g) ground almonds	1 tablespoonful ground almonds
¾ oz (20 g) carob powder	2 tablespoonsful carob powder
Vanilla Poached Pears:	*Vanilla Poached Pears:*
5 firm, ripe pears	5 firm, ripe pears
Juice of 1 lemon	Juice of 1 lemon
¾ pint (425 ml) water	2 cupsful water
3 oz (85 g) raw cane sugar	½ cupful raw cane sugar
1 vanilla pod, split lengthways	1 vanilla bean, split lengthways
Filling and Decoration:	*Filling and Decoration:*
Vanilla Custard Filling (page 177)	Vanilla Custard Filling (page 177)
1 oz (30 g) flaked almonds, lightly toasted	¼ cupful slivered almonds, lightly toasted
1 kiwi fruit	1 kiwi fruit
1-2 tablespoonsful pure maple syrup	1-2 tablespoonsful pure maple syrup

1. To prepare the cake, whisk the egg yolks and Vanilla Sugar together until the mixture lightens and becomes thick and creamy.

2. Mix the flour, ground almonds and carob powder together, combining them well.

3. In a separate bowl, whisk the egg whites until they stand in stiff peaks, then carefully fold into the egg yolk mixture, incorporating alternately with the dry ingredients, and beginning and ending with the whisked egg whites. Fold in the ingredients as carefully and as lightly as possible, so that the whites retain as much of their volume as possible, to give a meltingly light cake.

4. Pour the mixture into a greased 9 inch (23cm) round, deep cake tin and bake at 375°F/190°C (Gas Mark 5) for 35-40 minutes, or until the cake is nicely risen and firm to the touch.

5. Peel, core and halve the pears, then brush all over with lemon juice to prevent discolouration. Bring the water and sugar to the boil, stirring constantly until all the sugar has dissolved, then lower the heat to simmering point. Add the pear halves and vanilla pod to the simmering water, then poach for 10-15 minutes, or until the pears are tender but not too soft or in any way disintegrating. Lift the pears out of the cooking juices with a slotted spoon and set aside to cool.

6. Prepare the Vanilla Custard Filling as indicated. Slice the carob cake in half and spread a small amount of the custard filling over the uppermost part of the cake. Dice three of the pear halves into small chunks and fold into the remaining custard filling. Sandwich the cake together with the filling.

7. Arrange the remaining pear halves on top of the cake and sprinkle some toasted almonds in between each piece of fruit.

8. Cut the kiwi fruit into slices and place in the centre of the gâteau. Just before serving, brush the pear halves with some pure maple syrup, to give them a glistening surface.

CAROB AND STRAWBERRY GÂTEAU

Serves 6-8

A superb summer gâteau, covered with glazed strawberries and filled with a strawberry, orange and passion fruit filling.

Imperial (Metric)	American
4 eggs	4 eggs
4oz (115g) Vanilla Sugar (page 189)	⅔ cupful Vanilla Sugar (page 189)
3½oz (100g) wholemeal flour	¾ cupful + 1 tablespoonful wholewheat flour
¾oz (20g) carob powder	2 tablespoonsful carob powder
¾oz (20g) polyunsaturated margarine, melted and cooled	2 tablespoonsful polyunsaturated margarine, melted and cooled

Filling and Topping:	*Filling and Topping:*
Orange and Passion Fruit Custard Filling (page 180)	Orange and Passion Fruit Custard Filling (page 180)
1 lb (455g) strawberries, hulled and rinsed	3 cupsful strawberries, hulled and rinsed
Pure maple syrup	Pure maple syrup
Fresh strawberry or other leaves	Fresh strawberry or other leaves

1. Whisk the eggs and Vanilla Sugar together until thick, creamy and tripled in volume.

2. When the mixture reaches this consistency, carefully fold in the flour and carob powder, adding alternately with the melted margarine. Incorporate the ingredients as lightly and as quickly as possible, so that the mixture retains as much of its volume as possible, resulting in a deliciously light cake.

3. Pour the mixture into a greased 8 inch (20cm) round, deep cake tin, and bake at 375°F/190°C (Gas Mark 5)

for 30-35 minutes, until nicely risen and firm to the touch.

4. Meanwhile, prepare the Orange and Passion Fruit Custard Filling by the indicated method. Slice the carob cake in half and spread a thin coating of the custard filling over the top of the cake.

5. Dice half the quantity of fresh strawberries into quarter pieces and fold into the Orange and Passion Fruit Custard Filling. Now sandwich the carob cake together with the fruit and custard filling.

6. Cut the remaining strawberries into halves and arrange on top of the gâteau, cut-side-downwards. Using a pastry brush, brush the strawberries all over with pure maple syrup to glaze, and complete the gâteau by decorating with some fresh strawberry or other small leaves, dotting here and there on top of the gâteau, amidst the strawberries.

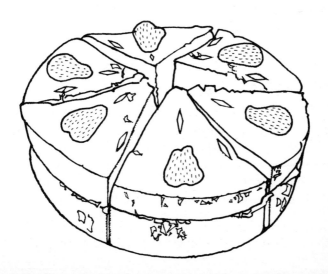

APPLE MERINGUES WITH CAROB SAUCE

Serves 4

Vanilla poached apples are encased in meringue, coated with a carob cream sauce and sprinkled with toasted almonds to make this special dessert.

Imperial (Metric)	American
Vanilla-Poached Apples:	*Vanilla-Poached Apples:*
4 large dessert apples	4 large dessert apples
Juice of 1 lemon	Juice of 1 lemon
¾ pint (425 ml) water	2 cupsful water
2 oz (55 g) raw cane sugar	⅓ cupful raw cane sugar
1 vanilla pod, split lengthways	1 vanilla bean, split lengthways
Meringue:	*Meringue:*
2 egg whites	2 egg whites
4 oz (115 g) light Muscovado sugar	⅔ cupful light Muscovado sugar
To Serve and Decorate:	*To Serve and Decorate:*
Carob and Vanilla Cream Sauce (page 184)	Carob and Vanilla Cream Sauce (page 184)
2 oz (55 g) flaked almonds, lightly toasted	½ cupful slivered almonds, lightly toasted

1. Peel and core the apples, leaving whole, then brush all over with lemon juice to prevent the fruit from discolouring.

2. Bring the water and sugar to the boil, stirring constantly until all the sugar has dissolved, then lower the heat to simmering point and add the apples and vanilla pod. Cover the saucepan with a lid and poach gently for about 15 minutes, or until the fruit is tender but not too soft or in any way disintegrating.

3. Use a slotted spoon to transfer the apples to an

ovenproof dish, after the poaching time.

4. To make the meringue, whisk the egg whites until they stand in stiff peaks. Add half the quantity of sugar, then continue whisking until the whites regain their former stiffness. Now carefully fold in the remaining sugar.

5. Pipe or spoon the meringue over the poached apples, covering completely, then bake at 300°F/150°C (Gas Mark 2) for 15-20 minutes, until the meringue is lightly browned.

6. Prepare the Carob Cream Sauce as indicated and pour over the apples just before serving. Complete with a sprinkling of lightly toasted flaked almonds.

3.
FANCY CAKES AND NOVELTY CAKES

Here are some delightful cakes that are especially appealing to children. For afternoon tea or for parties, children will love to have such novelty cakes as Butterflies, Top Hats, Coconut Owls and Funny Faces. For birthday celebrations, larger novelty cakes such as the Carob Clock Cake or the brightly coloured Merry-Go-Round Cake will delight your children.

BASIC MIXTURE FOR CAROB FANCY CAKES

Makes 12-15

Imperial (Metric)	American
4 oz (115 g) polyunsaturated margarine	½ cupful polyunsaturated margarine
3 oz (85 g) raw cane sugar	½ cupful raw cane sugar
2 eggs, lightly beaten	2 eggs, lightly beaten
4 oz (115 g) wholemeal flour	1 cupful wholewheat flour
1 oz (30 g) carob powder	¼ cupful carob powder
1½ teaspoonsful baking powder	1½ teaspoonsful baking powder
1 tablespoonful natural yogurt or milk	1 tablespoonful natural yogurt or milk

1. Cream the margarine and sugar together until light and fluffy.

2. Gradually incorporate the beaten eggs, adding a little at a time.

3. Fold in the flour, carob powder and baking powder. Now incorporate the natural yogurt or milk, to give a soft dropping consistency.

4. Spoon the mixture into individual paper cases and bake at 350°F/180°C (Gas Mark 4) for 12-15 minutes, until nicely risen and firm to the touch.

CAROB BUTTERFLIES

Imperial (Metric)	American
1 quantity basic Carob Fancy Cake mixture (page 82)	1 quantity basic Carob Fancy Cake mixture (page 82)
¼ pint (140 ml) double cream, chilled and stiffly whipped for piping	⅔ cupful heavy cream, chilled and stiffly whipped for piping

1. Prepare a batch of Carob Fancy Cakes, following the method given on page 82.

2. When cool, slice the top off each cake, using a sharp knife, and cut the top in half.

3. Pipe a swirl of whipped cream onto the centre of each cake and replace the two halves on top to form butterfly wings.

CAROB MADELEINES

Makes 12-15

These little dome-shaped carob cakes are flavoured with orange zest, coated with desiccated coconut and topped with chunks of natural dried pineapple.

Imperial (Metric)	American
4 oz (115 g) polyunsaturated margarine	½ cupful polyunsaturated margarine
3 oz (85 g) raw cane sugar	½ cupful raw cane sugar
Finely grated zest of 1 orange	Finely grated zest of 1 orange
2 eggs, lightly beaten	2 eggs, lightly beaten
4 oz (115 g) wholemeal flour	1 cupful wholewheat flour
1 oz (30 g) carob powder	¼ cupful carob powder
1½ teaspoonsful baking powder	1½ teaspoonsful baking powder
1 tablespoonful natural yogurt or milk	1 tablespoonful natural yogurt or milk

Coating:	*Coating:*
2-3 tablespoonsful clear honey or pure maple syrup	2-3 tablespoonsful clear honey or pure maple syrup
2 oz (55 g) desiccated coconut	⅔ cupful desiccated coconut
12-15 natural dried pineapple chunks	12-15 natural dried pineapple chunks

1. Cream the margarine, raw cane sugar and grated orange zest together until light and fluffy.

2. Gradually incorporate the beaten eggs, adding a little at a time.

3. Now fold in the flour, carob powder and baking powder, adding the natural yogurt or milk to give a soft dropping consistency.

4. Spoon the mixture into well-greased dariole moulds,

filling about three-quarters full, to allow room for the Madeleines to rise whilst baking.

5. Place the dariole moulds on a baking sheet and bake at 375°F/190°C (Gas Mark 5) for 15-20 minutes, until nicely risen and firm to the touch. Test by inserting a fine skewer into the cakes; if the skewer comes out clean, the Madeleines are cooked through.

6. When cooled, coat the Madeleines in clear honey or pure maple syrup, then roll in desiccated coconut, making sure that the cakes are fully covered with the coconut. Top each Madeleine with a chunk of natural dried pineapple, secured with a little clear honey or pure maple syrup.

CAROB BANANA BASKETS

Makes 12-15

Your children will love these basket-shaped carob cakes, filled with bananas and glazed with maple syrup.

Imperial (Metric)
4 oz (115 g) polyunsaturated margarine
2 oz (55 g) raw cane sugar
1 tablespoonful clear honey
2 eggs, lightly beaten
5 oz (140 g) wholemeal flour
1 oz (30 g) carob powder
1½ teaspoonsful baking powder
1 tablespoonful natural yogurt or milk

Decoration:
2 bananas, peeled and sliced into rounds
2-3 tablespoonsful pure maple syrup or clear honey
Piece of angelica, approximately 6 inches (15 cm) in length

American
½ cupful polyunsaturated margarine
⅓ cupful raw cane sugar
1 tablespoonful clear honey
2 eggs, lightly beaten
1¼ cupsful wholewheat flour
¼ cupful carob powder
1½ teaspoonsful baking powder
1 tablespoonful natural yogurt or milk

Decoration:
2 bananas, peeled and sliced into rounds
2-3 tablespoonsful pure maple syrup or clear honey
Piece of angelica, approximately 6 inches in length

1. Cream the margarine, raw cane sugar and honey together until pale and fluffy.

2. Gradually add the beaten eggs, incorporating a little at a time, then fold in the flour, carob powder and baking powder, adding the natural yogurt or milk to give a soft dropping consistency.

3. Spoon the mixture into individual paper cases and bake at 350°F/180°C (Gas Mark 4) for 12-15 minutes, until nicely risen and firm to the touch.

4. When the cakes have cooled, arrange the banana slices on top of them and glaze with pure maple syrup or clear honey.

5. Cut the angelica into thin strips and soak in warm water to make them pliable. Bend the soaked angelica strips to form the shape of basket handles. Stick the two ends of each strip of angelica into the cakes, making sure that the 'handles' are firmly implanted.

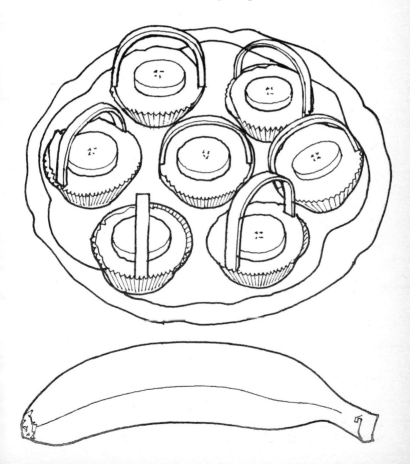

CAROB CLOCK CAKE

Serves 8

This is an ideal children's birthday cake – the two layers of carob and vanilla flavoured sponge are sandwiched together with a vanilla custard filling, and then coated with a dark and glossy melted carob coating. The top of the cake is decorated to represent a clock, with the clock hands positioned in accordance with the child's age.

Imperial (Metric)	American
6 oz (170g) polyunsaturated margarine	¾ cupful polyunsaturated margarine
4 oz (115g) Vanilla Sugar (page 189)	⅔ cupful Vanilla Sugar (page 189)
3 eggs, lightly beaten	3 eggs, lightly beaten
5 oz (140g) wholemeal flour	1¼ cupsful wholewheat flour
1 oz (30g) carob powder	¼ cupful carob powder
2 teaspoonsful baking powder	2 teaspoonsful baking powder
1 tablespoonful natural yogurt or milk	1 tablespoonful natural yogurt or milk

Filling:	*Filling:*
Vanilla Custard Filling (page 177)	Vanilla Custard Filling (page 177)

Coating and Decoration:	
Plain Carob Coating (page 183)	Plain Carob Coating (page 183)
3 fl oz (90ml) double cream, chilled and stiffly whipped for piping	⅓ cupful heavy cream, chilled and stiffly whipped for piping

1. To make the cake, cream the margarine and Vanilla Sugar together until light and fluffy.

2. Gradually incorporate the beaten eggs, adding a little at a time, then fold in the flour, carob powder and baking powder, adding the natural yogurt or milk to give a soft dropping consistency.

3. Spoon the mixture into two greased 7 inch (18cm) round cake tins, smoothing over the top, then bake at 375°F/190°C (Gas Mark 5) for 20-25 minutes, until the cakes are nicely risen and firm to the touch.

4. Prepare the Vanilla Custard Filling by the indicated method, then use the filling to sandwich the two cakes together.

5. Spread the carob coating evenly over the top of the cake and leave to set.

6. Spoon the whipped cream into a piping bag fitted with a fine writing nozzle and pipe numbers from one to twelve on the outer edge of the cake, to represent the numbers on the clock. Pipe two straight lines to represent the clock hands, with the long hand pointing to twelve and the short hand pointing to the number representing the child's age. Pipe a small rosette in the centre of the cake, where the two hands meet.

CAROB COCONUT OWLS

Makes 12-15

Imperial (Metric)
4 oz (115 g) polyunsaturated
   margarine
3 oz (115 g) Vanilla Sugar
   (page 189)
2 eggs, lightly beaten
4 oz (115 g) wholemeal flour
1 oz (30 g) carob powder
1½ teaspoonsful baking
   powder

Decoration:
2-3 tablespoonsful clear honey
   or pure maple syrup
4 oz (115 g) desiccated coconut

2 oz (55 g) small raisins
Small pieces dried apricot

American
½ cupful polyunsaturated
   margarine
½ cupful Vanilla Sugar
   (page 189)
2 eggs, lightly beaten
1 cupful wholewheat flour
¼ cupful carob powder
1½ teaspoonsful baking
   powder

Decoration:
2-3 tablespoonsful clear honey
   or pure maple syrup
1⅓ cupsful desiccated
   coconut
⅓ cupful small raisins
Small pieces dried apricot

1. Cream the margarine and Vanilla Sugar together until pale and fluffy.

2. Gradually incorporate the beaten eggs, adding a little at a time.

3. Fold in the flour, carob powder and baking powder, blending to a soft dropping consistency.

4. Spoon the mixture into well-greased dariole moulds, allowing some space for the cakes to rise whilst baking.

5. Stand the moulds on a baking sheet and bake at 375°F/190°C (Gas Mark 5) for 15-20 minutes, until nicely risen and firm to the touch. (Test the cakes by inserting a fine skewer into them; if the skewer comes

out clean, they are ready to be taken out of the oven.)

6. When the cakes have cooled, coat each one with clear honey or pure maple syrup, then roll in desiccated coconut. To make the eyes for the owls, stick two raisins onto each of the cakes, securing with some clear honey. Place small pieces of dried apricot just below the eyes to form a beak for the owls.

CAROB FRUIT FANCIES

Imperial (Metric)
1 quantity basic Carob Fancy Cake mixture (page 82)
¼ pint (140ml) double cream, chilled and stiffly whipped for piping
12-15 fresh cherries, strawberries, raspberries or chunks of fresh pineapple

American
1 quantity basic Carob Fancy Cake mixture (page 82)
⅔ cupful heavy cream, chilled and stiffly whipped for piping
12-15 fresh cherries, strawberries, raspberries or chunks of fresh pineaple

1. Prepare a batch of Carob Fancy Cakes, following the indicated method.

2. Pipe a decorative swirl of whipped cream in the centre of each cake and top with a fresh cherry or any other fresh fruit.

FUNNY FACES

Makes 12-15

These small carob cakes are given a glossy carob coating and funny smiling faces.

Imperial (Metric)	American
4 oz (115g) polyunsaturated margarine	½ cupful polyunsaturated margarine
2 oz (55g) raw cane sugar	⅓ cupful raw cane sugar
1 tablespoonful clear honey	1 tablespoonful clear honey
2 eggs, lightly beaten	2 eggs, lightly beaten
4 oz (115g) wholemeal flour	1 cupful wholewheat flour
1 oz (30g) carob powder	¼ cupful carob powder
1½ teaspoonsful baking powder	1½ teaspoonsful baking powder
1 tablespoonful natural yogurt or milk	1 tablespoonful natural yogurt or milk

Coating and Decoration:	*Coating and Decoration:*
Plain Carob Coating (page 183)	Plain Carob Coating (page 183)
Small raisins	Small raisins
Small strips of dried apricot or pineapple	Small strips of dried apricot or pineapple
Nibbed almonds	Nibbed almonds

1. Cream the margarine, raw cane sugar and honey together until light and fluffy.

2. Gradually incorporate the beaten eggs, adding a little at a time and beating well after each addition.

3. Now fold in the flour, carob powder and baking powder, adding a little natural yogurt or milk to give a soft dropping consistency.

4. Spoon the mixture into small paper cases and bake at 350°F/180°C (Gas Mark 4) for 12-15 minutes, until

nicely risen and firm to the touch.

5. Allow the cakes to cool, then spread the carob coating
   evenly on top. Before the coating sets, give the cakes
   funny faces, using raisins for the eyes, strips of dried
   apricot or pineapple for the nose and nibbed almonds
   for the mouth and eyebrows.

CAROB TOP HATS

Imperial (Metric)
1 quantity basic Carob Fancy
  Cake mixture (page 82)
¼ pint (140ml) double cream,
  chilled and stiffly whipped
  for piping

American
1 quantity basic Carob Fancy
  Cake mixture (page 82)
⅔ cupful heavy cream, chilled
  and stiffly whipped for
  piping

1. Prepare a batch of Carob Fancy Cakes, following the
   indicated method.

2. Using a sharp knife, hollow out a small piece from the
   centre of each cake and fill the hollow with a swirl of
   piped whipped cream. Replace the cut piece on top of
   the cream, to form a top hat.

CAROB MERINGUE BOATS

Makes 6-8

Imperial (Metric)	American
3 egg whites	3 egg whites
5 oz (140g) light Muscovado sugar	1 cupful light Muscovado sugar
1 oz (30g) carob powder	¼ cupful carob powder

Decoration:	*Decoration:*
¼ pint (140ml) double cream, stiffly whipped for piping	⅔ cupful heavy cream, stiffly whipped for piping
8 oz (225g) strawberries, hulled and rinsed	2 cupsful strawberries, hulled and rinsed
Coloured paper/glue	Coloured paper/glue
Wooden cocktail sticks	Wooden cocktail sticks

1. Whisk the egg whites until they stand in stiff peaks.

2. Add half the quantity of Muscovado sugar to the whites, then continue whisking until the whites regain their former stiffness.

3. Carefully fold in the remaining Muscovado sugar and carob powder, then spoon the mixture into a piping bag fitted with a large star nozzle.

4. Pipe oval boat-shaped meringues onto a baking sheet lined with waxed paper or greased greaseproof paper and bake at 250°F/130°C (Gas Mark ½) for about 2 hours, until the meringues are crisp and dry.

5. When cool, fill the meringue boats with some decoratively piped whipped cream and top with fresh strawberries.

6. Make sails or flags for the boats by sticking some pieces of coloured paper onto wooden cocktail sticks. Place one of the sails or flags in the centre of each meringue

boat. Serve as soon as possible whilst the meringue is
crisp.

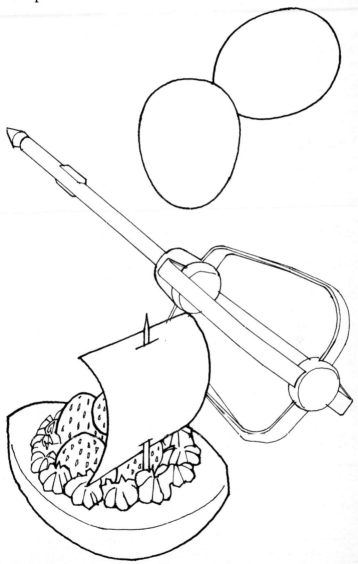

CAROB MERRY-GO-ROUND CAKE

Serves 8-10

A most attractive carob-coated novelty cake, decorated with animal-shaped biscuits holding coloured ribbons on a merry-go-round.

Imperial (Metric)	American
8 oz (225 g) polyunsaturated margarine	1 cupful polyunsaturated margarine
6 oz (170 g) raw cane sugar	1 cupful raw cane sugar
Finely grated zest of 1 orange	Finely grated zest of 1 orange
1 tablespoonful clear honey	1 tablespoonful clear honey
3 eggs, lightly beaten	3 eggs, lightly beaten
7 oz (200 g) wholemeal flour	1¾ cupsful wholewheat flour
1 oz (30 g) carob powder	¼ cupful carob powder
3 teaspoonsful baking powder	3 teaspoonsful baking powder
1 tablespoonful natural yogurt or milk	1 tablespoonful natural yogurt or milk

Filling and Decoration:	*Filling and Decoration:*
Raw cane sugar raspberry jam or thick honey	Raw cane sugar raspberry jelly or thick honey
Plain Carob Coating (page 183)	Plain Carob Coating (page 183)
Long meat skewer	Long meat skewer
Different coloured ribbons	Different coloured ribbons
Plain Animal Biscuits (page 129)	Plain Animal Biscuits (page 129)
2 tablespoonsful stiffly whipped double cream	2 tablespoonsful stiffly whipped heavy cream

1. Cream the margarine, raw cane sugar, finely grated orange zest and honey together until pale and fluffy.

2. Gradually incorporate the beaten eggs, adding a little at a time and beating well after each addition.

3. Now fold in the flour, carob powder and baking powder, together with sufficient natural yogurt or milk

to give a soft dropping consistency.

4. Spoon the mixture into two greased 8 inch (20cm) round cake tins, smoothing over the top, then bake at 375°F/190°C (Gas Mark 5) for about 25 minutes, until the cakes are nicely risen and firm to the touch.

5. When cool, sandwich the cakes together with some raspberry jam or thick honey.

6. Spread the carob coating evenly all over the cake, covering completely, then before the coating sets, press a circle of animal biscuits around the side of the cake.

7. Cover a meat skewer with different coloured ribbons, allowing each piece of ribbon to overhang by about 12 inches (30cm) from the top of the skewer so that the ribbons can fall over the cake to make the merry-go-round. You should have the same number of ribbons as animal biscuits. Place the skewer firmly into the centre of the cake, giving each animal a piece of ribbon.

8. Complete the cake by decorating with a small amount of decoratively piped whipped cream.

4.

BISCUITS AND TRAY CAKES

Here are lots of ideas for tasty wholemeal biscuits and tray cakes, made with whole grains, carob, nuts, dried fruits and other natural ingredients. They make nutritive, fibre-rich, natural snacks and are also ideal for including in a wholefood lunch box.

   Biscuits and tray cakes are quick and easy to make and are always immensely popular with the family. Always store your wholemeal biscuits in an airtight container, to help them to retain their crispness.

CAROB CHIP BISCUITS

Makes 25-30

These crunchy wholewheat biscuits are flavoured with a subtle hint of vanilla and dotted with dark and tasty carob chips.

Imperial (Metric)	American
4 oz (115 g) polyunsaturated margarine	½ cupful polyunsaturated margarine
4 oz (115 g) Vanilla Sugar (page 189)	⅔ cupful Vanilla Sugar (page 189)
1 egg, lightly beaten	1 egg, lightly beaten
7 oz (200 g) wholemeal flour	1¾ cupsful wholewheat flour
1 oz (30 g) ground almonds	¼ cupful ground almonds
1 teaspoonful baking powder	1 teaspoonful baking powder

2 x 2½oz (75g) carob bars;
   coarsely diced into chips
1-2 tablespoonsful milk

2 x 2½oz carob bars;
   coarsely diced into chips
1-2 tablespoonsful milk

1. Cream the margarine and Vanilla Sugar together until pale and fluffy.

2. Gradually incorporate the beaten egg, adding a little at a time.

3. Now fold in the flour, ground almonds, baking powder and carob chips, adding sufficient milk to give a fairly soft dropping consistency.

4. Drop heaped teaspoonsful of the mixture onto greased baking sheets, smoothing over with the back of the teaspoon and shaping into neat circles. Space the mixture well apart to allow room for the biscuits to spread whilst baking.

5. Bake the biscuits at 350°F/180°C (Gas Mark 4) for 12-15 minutes. Store the biscuits in an airtight container when cool.

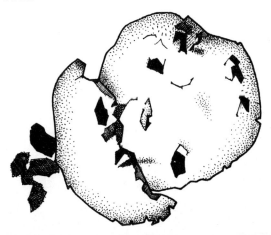

CAROB AND DATE COOKIES

Makes about 30

Imperial (Metric)	American
4 oz (115g) dates, stoned	1 cupful dates, stoned
6 oz (170g) wholemeal flour	1½ cupsful wholewheat flour
1 oz (30g) ground almonds	¼ cupful ground almonds
1½ teaspoonsful ground cinnamon	1½ teaspoonsful ground cinnamon
¼ teaspoonful bicarbonate of soda	¼ teaspoonful bicarbonate of soda
4 oz (115g) polyunsaturated margarine	½ cupful polyunsaturated margarine
1 oz (30g) carob powder	¼ cupful carob powder
3 oz (85g) Vanilla Sugar (page 189)	½ cupful Vanilla Sugar (page 189)
1 egg, lightly beaten	1 egg, lightly beaten
1 teaspoonful clear honey	1 teaspoonful clear honey
2 tablespoonsful milk	2 tablespoonsful milk

1. Soak the dates in boiling water for 2-3 minutes, in order to soften them. Drain the dates after the soaking period and dice into small pieces.

2. Place the flour, ground almonds, cinnamon and bicarbonate of soda in a mixing bowl, combining them well.

3. Rub the margarine into the dry ingredients, using the fingertips, until a breadcrumb consistency is obtained.

4. Now fold in the carob powder, Vanilla Sugar and diced dates, making sure that the dates are evenly distributed as they will tend to stick together in small clumps.

5. Make a well in the centre of the ingredients, then pour in the beaten egg and honey. Begin blending the ingredients together, adding sufficient milk to bind the

mixture to a fairly soft dough.

6. Drop heaped teaspoonsful of the mixture onto greased baking sheets, smoothing over with the back of the teaspoon and shaping into neat circles. Allow some space between the cookies, to enable them to spread whilst baking.

7. Bake at 350°F/180°C (Gas Mark 4) for about 15 minutes. Allow the cookies to cool thoroughly, then store in an airtight container.

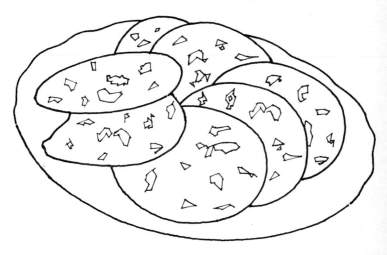

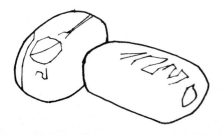

CAROB AND ORANGE BISCUITS

Makes about 30

The flavour of freshly grated orange zest penetrates these dark and delicious carob biscuits.

Imperial (Metric)
4 oz (115 g) polyunsaturated margarine
4 oz (115 g) raw cane sugar
Finely grated zest of 1 orange
1 egg yolk
8 oz (225 g) wholemeal flour
1 oz (30 g) carob powder
¼ teaspoonful bicarbonate of soda
Strained juice of ½ orange
About 30 split blanched almonds
Lightly beaten egg white, to glaze

American
½ cupful polyunsaturated margarine
⅔ cupful raw cane sugar
Finely grated zest of 1 orange
1 egg yolk
2 cupsful wholewheat flour
¼ cupful carob powder
¼ teaspoonful bicarbonate of soda
Strained juice of ½ orange
About 30 split blanched almonds
Lightly beaten egg white, to glaze

1. Cream the margarine, raw cane sugar and finely grated orange zest together until pale and fluffy.

2. Beat in the egg yolk, then fold in the flour, carob powder and bicarbonate of soda, adding alternately with the strained orange juice and blending to a stiff consistency.

3. Turn the mixture onto a lightly floured board and roll out to a thickness of about ¼ inch (6 mm). Cut into rounds with a 2 inch (5 cm) fluted biscuit cutter and place on lightly greased baking sheets.

4. Press a split blanched almond on top of each biscuit, then brush all over with lightly beaten egg white to glaze.

5. Bake the biscuits at 350°F/180°C (Gas Mark 4) for about 15 minutes. Allow to cool thoroughly, then store in an airtight container.

CAROB MACAROONS

Makes about 10

Flavoured with carob and almonds, these tasty little biscuits are soft on the inside, with a crisp outer coating.

Imperial (Metric)	American
1 egg white	1 egg white
2 oz (55g) ground almonds	½ cupful ground almonds
1 oz (30g) carob powder	¼ cupful carob powder
1 oz (30g) light Muscovado sugar	2 tablespoonsful light Muscovado sugar
½ teaspoonful almond essence	½ teaspoonful almond essence
Whole blanched almonds	Whole blanched almonds

1. Whisk the egg white until it stands in stiff peaks.

2. Fold the ground almonds, carob powder, Muscovado sugar and almond essence into the egg white, blending to a soft, smooth consistency.

3. Line two baking sheets with rice paper and drop heaped teaspoonsful of the mixture onto the rice paper, spacing well apart to allow room for the mixture to spread whilst in the oven.

4. Place a whole blanched almond in the centre of each macaroon, then bake at 350°F/180°C (Gas Mark 4) for 15-20 minutes, until firm to the touch.

5. Allow the macaroons to cool, then trim off the excess rice paper. Store in an airtight container.

CAROB AND HAZELNUT BISCUITS

Makes about 30

Roasted ground hazelnuts are combined with carob powder, sultanas and other natural ingredients to make these flavour-rich biscuits.

Imperial (Metric)	American
5 oz (140g) wholemeal flour	1¼ cupsful wholewheat flour
2 oz (55g) roasted ground hazelnuts	½ cupful roasted ground hazelnuts
¼ teaspoonful bicarbonate of soda	¼ teaspoonful bicarbonate of soda
4 oz (115g) polyunsaturated margarine	½ cupful polyunsaturated margarine
1 oz (30g) carob powder	¼ cupful carob powder
3 oz (85g) light Muscovado sugar	½ cupful light Muscovado sugar
2 oz (55g) sultanas, finely diced	⅓ cupful golden seedless raisins, finely diced
1 egg, lightly beaten	1 egg, lightly beaten
2 teaspoonsful clear honey	2 teaspoonsful clear honey
1-2 tablespoonsful milk	1-2 tablespoonsful milk
Lightly beaten egg white to glaze	Lightly beaten egg white to glaze

1. Place the flour, ground hazelnuts and bicarbonate of soda in a mixing bowl, combining them well.

2. Rub the margarine into the dry ingredients, until a breadcrumb consistency is obtained.

3. Fold in the carob powder, Muscovado sugar and diced sultanas, then make a well in the centre of the ingredients and pour in the beaten egg and honey. Begin blending the ingredients together, adding sufficient milk to bind the mixture to a fairly stiff, workable dough.

4. Turn out onto a lightly floured board and roll out to a thickness of about ¼ inch (6mm). Cut into rounds with a 2 inch (5cm) fluted biscuit cutter and place on lightly greased baking sheets.

5. Brush the biscuits all over with lightly beaten egg white, then bake at 350°F/180°C (Gas Mark 4) for about 15 minutes, until firm to the touch. Allow the biscuits to cool thoroughly, then store in an airtight container.

CAROB MUESLI BITES

Makes 15-18

Imperial (Metric)	American
4 oz (115 g) block carob	4 ounce block carob
2 oz (55 g) polyunsaturated margarine	¼ cupful polyunsaturated margarine
1 tablespoonful clear honey	1 tablespoonful clear honey
6 oz (170g) muesli	1½ cupsful muesli
2 oz (55 g) nibbed almonds	½ cupful nibbed almonds

1. Break the carob into pieces and place in a saucepan with the margarine. Set the saucepan over a gentle heat, until the carob and margarine are fully melted.

2. Away from the heat, stir the honey into the melted ingredients, blending well, then fold in the muesli and nibbed almonds.

3. Put teaspoonsful of the mixture into small fluted paper cases and place in the refrigerator to set.

CAROB BOURBONS

Makes about 20

Imperial (Metric)	American
4 oz (115g) polyunsaturated margarine	½ cupful polyunsaturated margarine
4 oz (115g) Vanilla Sugar (page 189)	⅔ cupful Vanilla Sugar (page 189)
1 egg, lightly beaten	1 egg, lightly beaten
8 oz (225g) wholemeal flour	2 cupsful wholewheat flour
1 oz (30g) carob powder	¼ cupful carob powder

Filling:	*Filling:*
1 x 2½ oz (75g) carob bar	1 x 2½ ounce carob bar

1. Cream the margarine and Vanilla Sugar together until pale and fluffy.

2. Gradually add the beaten egg, incorporating a little at a time, then fold in the flour and carob powder, blending to a fairly stiff consistency.

3. Turn the mixture out onto a lightly floured board and roll out to a thickness of about ⅛ inch (3mm). Cut the mixture into evenly sized rectangles measuring 1 inch x 3 inches (2.5cm x 7cm).

4. Transfer the biscuits to greased baking sheets and prick with a fork. Bake at 350°F/180°C (Gas Mark 4) for 10-12 minutes, until firm to the touch.

5. Meanwhile, break the carob bar into pieces and place in a heat-resistant bowl. Set the bowl over a saucepan of gently simmering water, to melt the carob. Blend a small quantity of water into the melted carob, to obtain a smooth and thick spreading consistency.

6. Allow the biscuits to cool thoroughly on a wire rack,

then sandwich together with the melted carob. Allow the carob filling to set, then store the biscuits in an airtight container.

CAROB OAT COOKIES

Makes about 30

The added fibre and goodness of oats is contained in these crunchy carob cookies.

Imperial (Metric)	American
4 oz (115 g) polyunsaturated margarine	½ cupful polyunsaturated margarine
3 oz (85 g) light Muscovado sugar	½ cupful light Muscovado sugar
1 egg, lightly beaten	1 egg, lightly beaten
4 oz (115 g) wholemeal flour	1 cupful wholewheat flour
1 oz (30 g) carob powder	¼ cupful carob powder
½ teaspoonful baking powder	½ teaspoonful baking powder
2 oz (55 g) porridge oats	½ cupful rolled oats

1. Cream the margarine and Muscovado sugar together until light and fluffy.

2. Gradually incorporate the beaten egg, adding a little at a time, then fold in the wholemeal flour, carob powder, baking powder and porridge oats, blending to a fairly soft dropping consistency.

3. Place heaped teaspoonsful of the mixture onto greased baking sheets, smoothing over with the back of the teaspoon and shaping into neat circles. Allow some space between the cookies to enable them to spread whilst in the oven.

4. Bake at 375°F/190°C (Gas Mark 5) for 10-12 minutes. Store the cookies in an airtight container when completely cool.

CAROB COATED DIGESTIVE BISCUITS

Makes about 20

The dark and glossy carob coating adds the finishing touch to these deliciously crunchy and nutritious two-grain biscuits.

Imperial (Metric)	American
6 oz (170g) wholemeal flour	1½ cupsful wholewheat flour
2 oz (55g) medium oatmeal	½ cupful medium oatmeal
¼ teaspoonful bicarbonate of soda	¼ teaspoonful bicarbonate of soda
4 oz (115g) polyunsaturated margarine	½ cupful polyunsaturated margarine
1 oz (30g) light Muscovado sugar	2 tablespoonsful light Muscovado sugar
1 egg yolk	1 egg yolk
1 teaspoonful clear honey	1 teaspoonful clear honey
1-2 tablespoonsful milk	1-2 tablespoonsful milk
Lightly beaten egg white, to glaze	Lightly beaten egg white, to glaze

Coating: *Coating:*
Plain Carob Coating (page 183)   Plain Carob Coating (page 183)

1. Place the flour, oatmeal and bicarbonate of soda in a mixing bowl, combining them well.

2. Using the fingertips, rub the margarine into the dry ingredients until a breadcrumb consistency is obtained.

3. Fold in the Muscovado sugar, then incorporate the egg yolk and honey, together with sufficient milk to bind the ingredients to a stiff, workable dough.

4. Turn the mixture out onto a lightly floured board and roll out to a thickness of about ¼ inch (6mm). Cut into rounds with a plain biscuit cutter, then transfer the biscuits to lightly greased baking sheets.

5. Brush the biscuits all over with lightly beaten egg white, then bake at 350°F/180°C (Gas Mark 4) for 15-20 minutes, until golden brown.

6. Allow the biscuits to cool thoroughly, then spread the Carob Coating over the underside of the biscuits. Leave the coating to set, then store the digestives in an airtight container.

CAROB COCONUT COOKIES

Makes 10-12

Imperial (Metric)	American
2 egg whites	2 egg whites
3 oz (85 g) Vanilla Sugar (page 189)	½ cupful Vanilla Sugar (page 189)
1 oz (30g) carob powder	¼ cupful carob powder
6 oz (170g) desiccated coconut	2 cupsful desiccated coconut
Decoration:	*Decoration:*
Dried pineapple pieces	Dried pineapple pieces
Clear honey	Clear honey

1. Whisk the egg whites until they stand in stiff peaks. Fold in the Vanilla Sugar, then continue whisking until the whites become once again stiff and thick.

2. Now fold in the carob powder and desiccated coconut, then drop heaped teaspoonsful of the mixture onto baking sheets lined with rice paper, allowing some space for the cookies to spread whilst in the oven.

3. Bake at 300°F/150°C (Gas Mark 2) for about 40 minutes, until firm to the touch.

4. Decorate the cookies with small pieces of dried pineapple, secured with a little clear honey. Store the cookies in an airtight container when completely cool.

CAROB FRUIT AND NUT COOKIES

Makes about 20

Imperial (Metric)	American
3 oz (85 g) polyunsaturated margarine	⅓ cupful polyunsaturated margarine
2 oz (55 g) Vanilla Sugar (page 189)	⅓ cupful Vanilla Sugar (page 189)
1 egg, lightly beaten	1 egg, lightly beaten
5 oz (140 g) wholemeal flour	1¼ cupsful wholewheat flour
1 oz (30 g) ground almonds	¼ cupful ground almonds
½ oz (30 g) carob powder	1 tablespoonful carob powder
½ teaspoonful baking powder	½ teaspoonful baking powder
1 oz (30 g) nibbed almonds	¼ cupful nibbed almonds
2 oz (55 g) raisins, finely chopped	⅓ cupful raisins, finely chopped
1 tablespoonful milk	1 tablespoonful milk

1. Cream the margarine and Vanilla Sugar together until pale and fluffy.

2. Gradually add the beaten egg, then fold in the flour, ground almonds, carob powder and baking powder.

3. Stir in the nibbed almonds and chopped raisins, and if necessary, incorporate a little milk to produce a soft dropping consistency.

4. Drop heaped teaspoonsful of the mixture onto greased baking sheets, smoothing over with the back of the teaspoon and shaping into neat circles. Space the mixture well apart to allow room for the biscuits to spread whilst baking.

5. Bake at 350°F/180°C (Gas Mark 4) for 12-15 minutes. Store the cookies in an airtight container when cool.

CAROB AND ALMOND SLICES

Cuts into 18 slices

A dark and crunchy biscuit base is covered with flaked almonds to make these deliciously nutty slices.

Imperial (Metric)	American
4 oz (115 g) polyunsaturated margarine	½ cupful polyunsaturated margarine
2 oz (55 g) raw cane sugar	⅓ cupful raw cane sugar
6 oz (170 g) wholemeal flour	1½ cupsful wholewheat flour
2 oz (55 g) carob powder	½ cupful carob powder
1 egg white, lightly beaten	1 egg white, lightly beaten
2-3 oz (55-85 g) flaked almonds	¼-½ cupful slivered almonds

1. Cream the margarine and raw cane sugar together until pale and fluffy.

2. Fold the flour and carob powder into the creamed mixture, blending to a stiff consistency. If the mixture becomes too stiff, add a small amount of milk to give a more workable consistency.

3. Press the mixture into a greased Swiss roll tin measuring 11 x 7 inches (28 x 18 cm), spreading evenly with a palette knife.

4. Brush all over the surface of the biscuit base with the lightly beaten egg white, then sprinkle with the flaked almonds.

5. Bake at 350°F/180°C (Gas Mark 4) for about 20 minutes, until the biscuit base is firm to the touch and the almonds golden brown.

6. Mark into slices whilst still warm, but leave to cool thoroughly before removing from the baking tin. Store the slices in an airtight container.

CAROB COATED FLORENTINES

Makes 12-15

Imperial (Metric)
4 oz (115 g) polyunsaturated margarine
4 oz (115 g) Vanilla Sugar (page 189)
2 oz (55 g) nibbed almonds
1 oz (30 g) flaked almonds
1 oz (30 g) sultanas, diced
1 oz (30 g) dried pineapple, diced
1 oz (30 g) dried apricots, diced

Coating:
Plain Carob Coating (page 183)

American
½ cupful polyunsaturated margarine
⅔ cupful Vanilla Sugar (page 189)
½ cupful nibbed almonds
¼ cupful slivered almonds
¼ cupful golden seedless raisins, diced
¼ cupful dried pineapple, diced
¼ cupful dried apricots, diced

Coating:
Plain Carob Coating (page 183)

1. Line three baking sheets with non-stick paper.

2. Melt the margarine in a saucepan set over a moderate heat. Add the Vanilla Sugar, blending well, then bring slowly to the boil. Allow the mixture to boil for 1 minute.

3. Remove from the heat and allow to cool slightly, then stir in the nibbed and flaked almonds, sultanas, pineapple and apricots.

4. Place teaspoonsful of the mixture onto the lined baking sheets, flattening with a palette knife and shaping into neat circles. Space the mixture well apart to allow room for the Florentines to spread whilst in the oven.

5. Bake at 350°F/180°C (Gas Mark 4) for about 10 minutes, until golden brown. Allow the Florentines to cool, then carefully remove from the lining paper.

6. Prepare the Carob Coating as indicated and spread over the smooth side of the Florentines. When the Carob Coating begins to set, mark lines across the coating with a fork, to make a swirly pattern. Allow to set thoroughly, then store the Florentines in an airtight container.

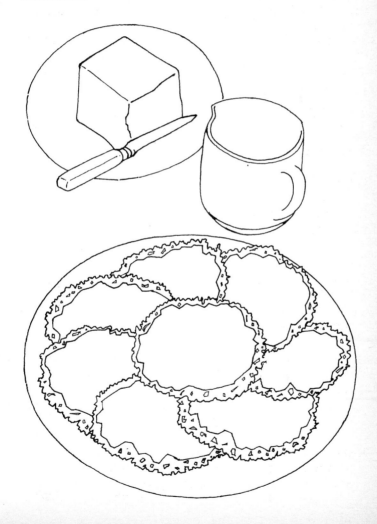

CAROB HONEY AND SULTANA SQUARES

Cuts into 16 squares

Imperial (Metric)	American
3 oz (85 g) sultanas	½ cupful golden seedless raisins
6 oz (170 g) wholemeal flour	1½ cupsful wholewheat flour
1 oz (30 g) ground almonds	¼ cupful ground almonds
1 oz (30 g) carob powder	¼ cupful carob powder
½ oz (15 g) Vanilla Sugar (page 189)	1 tablespoonful Vanilla Sugar (page 189)
Finely grated zest of 1 orange	Finely grated zest of 1 orange
1 teaspoonful bicarbonate of soda	1 teaspoonful bicarbonate of soda
4 oz (115 g) polyunsaturated margarine	½ cupful polyunsaturated margarine
2 tablespoonsful honey	2 tablespoonsful honey
1-2 tablespoonsful natural yogurt or milk	1-2 tablespoonsful natural yogurt or milk

Decoration:	*Decoration:*
Whole pecans	Whole pecans
Clear honey	Clear honey

1. Cover the sultanas with boiling water and leave to soak for 8-10 minutes, in order to make them soft and plump. Drain the sultanas after the softening period.

2. Place the flour, ground almonds, carob powder, Vanilla Sugar, finely grated orange zest and bicarbonate of soda in a mixing bowl, combining them well. Add the plumped sultanas to the dry ingredients.

3. Melt the margarine and honey together in a saucepan set over a moderate heat.

4. Make a well in the centre of the dry ingredients and pour in the melted margarine and honey. Begin blending the ingredients together, adding a sufficient amount of

natural yogurt or milk to give a soft dropping consistency.

5. Spoon the mixture into a greased 8 inch (20cm) square baking tin, smoothing over the top, then bake at 350°F/180°C (Gas Mark 4) for 25-30 minutes, until firm to the touch.

6. Allow to cool thoroughly in the baking tin, then cut into squares. Decorate the squares with some whole pecans, secured by spreading the underside of the nuts with some clear honey. Store the squares in an airtight container.

CAROB AND ALMOND SQUARES

Cuts into 16 squares

These tasty squares are made with a melted carob bar and are packed with almonds.

Imperial (Metric)	American
1 x 2½oz (75g) carob bar	1 x 2½ ounce carob bar
2oz (55g) polyunsaturated margarine	¼ cupful polyunsaturated margarine
4oz (115g) wholemeal flour	1 cupful wholewheat flour
1½ teaspoonsful baking powder	1½ teaspoonsful baking powder
2oz (55g) nibbed almonds	½ cupful nibbed almonds

Decoration:	*Decoration:*
Split blanched almonds, lightly toasted	Split blanched almonds, lightly toasted
Clear honey	Clear honey

1. Break the carob bar into pieces and place in a saucepan with the margarine. Set the saucepan over a low heat, until the carob and margarine are fully melted.

2. Remove from the heat and fold the flour and baking powder into the melted ingredients, blending well, then fold in the nibbed almonds.

3. Spoon the mixture into a greased 8 inch (20cm) square baking tin, smoothing over the top, then bake at 350°F/180°C (Gas Mark 4) for 35-40 minutes, until firm to the touch.

4. Allow to cool thoroughly in the baking tin, then cut into squares. Decorate with some toasted almonds, secured by spreading the underside of the nuts with some clear honey. Store in an airtight container.

CAROB CREAM SHELLS

Makes about 10

These attractive shell-shaped biscuits are sandwiched together with a soured cream filling.

Imperial (Metric)	American
4 oz (115 g) polyunsaturated margarine	½ cupful polyunsaturated margarine
4 oz (115 g) Vanilla Sugar (page 189)	⅔ cupful Vanilla Sugar (page 189)
1 egg, lightly beaten	1 egg, lightly beaten
6 oz (170 g) wholemeal flour	1½ cupsful wholewheat flour
½ oz (15 g) carob powder	1 tablespoon carob powder

Filling:
Soured Cream Filling (page 182)

Filling:
Soured Cream Filling (page 182)

1. Cream the margarine and Vanilla Sugar together until and fluffy.

2. Gradually add the beaten egg, then fold in the flour and carob powder.

3. Spread the mixture evenly into greased shell-shaped biscuit moulds, or using a piping bag fitted with a large star nozzle, pipe small shell shapes onto a greased baking sheet.

4. Bake the biscuits at 375°F/190°C (Gas Mark 5) for 12-15 minutes.

5. When cool, sandwich the shells together with the Soured Cream Filling (or with whipped double cream).

CAROB AND ALMOND BISCUITS

Makes about 30

These carob and almond flavoured biscuits have a crunchy, shortbread texture.

Imperial (Metric)	American
5 oz (140g) wholemeal flour	1¼ cupsful wholewheat flour
2 oz (55g) ground almonds	½ cupful ground almonds
1 oz (30g) carob powder	¼ cupful carob powder
3 oz (85g) light Muscovado sugar	½ cupful light Muscovado sugar
¼ teaspoonful bicarbonate of soda	¼ teaspoonful bicarbonate of soda
½ teaspoonful almond essence	½ teaspoonful almond essence
5 oz (140g) polyunsaturated margarine	½ cupful + 2½ tablespoonsful polyunsaturated margarine
1 teaspoonful clear honey	1 teaspoonful clear honey
About 30 whole blanched almonds	About 30 whole blanched almonds
Lightly beaten egg white, to glaze	Lightly beaten egg white, to glaze

1. Place the flour, ground almonds, carob powder, Muscovado sugar, bicarbonate of soda and almond essence in a mixing bowl, combining them well.

2. Using the fingertips, rub the margarine into the dry ingredients, then add the honey and knead the mixture to a stiff dough.

3. Roll out on a lightly floured board and cut into rounds with a fluted biscuit cutter.

4. Place the biscuits on greased baking sheets and press a whole blanched almond in the centre of each one.

5. Brush all over the surface of the biscuits and the

almonds with lightly beaten egg white, then bake at 350°F/180°C (Gas Mark 4) for about 15 minutes, until firm to the touch. Allow the biscuits to cool, then store in an airtight container.

CAROB RAISIN SQUARES

Cuts into 16 squares

Imperial (Metric)
4 oz (115 g) polyunsaturated margarine
3 oz (85 g) raw cane sugar
2 eggs, lightly beaten
6 oz (170 g) wholemeal flour
1 oz (30 g) carob powder
1½ teaspoonsful baking powder
4 oz (115 g) small raisins
1 tablespoonful natural yogurt or milk

Decoration:
Whole pecans or walnuts
Clear honey

American
½ cupful polyunsaturated margarine
½ cupful raw cane sugar
2 eggs, lightly beaten
1½ cupsful wholewheat flour
¼ cupful carob powder
1½ teaspoonsful baking powder
⅔ cupful small raisins
1 tablespoonful natural yogurt or milk

Decoration:
Whole pecans or English walnuts
Clear honey

1. Cream the margarine and raw cane sugar together until pale and fluffy.

2. Gradually incorporate the beaten eggs, adding a little at a time.

3. Fold in the flour, carob powder and baking powder. Now fold in the raisins, together with sufficient natural yogurt or milk to give a soft dropping consistency.

4. Spoon the mixture into a greased 8 inch (20 cm) square baking tin, spreading evenly, then bake at 350°F/180°C (Gas Mark 4) for 30-35 minutes, until firm to the touch.

5. Allow to cool in the baking tin, then cut into squares. Decorate each of the squares with a whole pecan or walnut, secured with a little clear honey.

CAROB WHEAT FLAKE CLUSTERS

Makes about 12

Imperial (Metric)	American
1 x 2½ oz (75g) carob bar	1 x 2½ ounce carob bar
2 oz (55g) wholewheat flakes	1¼ cupsful wholewheat flakes
2 oz (55g) nibbed almonds, lightly toasted	½ cupful nibbed almonds, lightly toasted

1. Break the carob bar into pieces and place in a heat-resistant bowl. Set the bowl over a saucepan of gently simmering water, to melt the carob.

2. Gradually blend some water into the melted carob, over the heat, adding a sufficient amount to give a smooth and thick coating consistency.

3. Mix the wheat flakes and toasted almonds together, then carefully fold into the melted carob, ensuring that the wheat flakes do not crumble and disintegrate.

4. Spoon the mixture in clusters onto waxed paper and leave to set. Serve the clusters in small fluted paper cases.

CAROB AND PINEAPPLE SLICES

Cuts into 18 slices

Natural dried pineapple is combined with carob powder, soured cream, almonds and other natural ingredients to make these most tasty slices.

Imperial (Metric)	American
9 oz (255g) wholemeal flour	2¼ cupsful wholewheat flour
1 teaspoonful bicarbonate of soda	1 teaspoonful bicarbonate of soda
4 oz (115g) polyunsaturated margarine	½ cupful polyunsaturated margarine
1 oz (30g) carob powder	¼ cupful carob powder
4 oz (115g) raw cane sugar	⅔ cupful raw cane sugar
4 oz (115g) dried pineapple, chopped	1 cupful dried pineapple, chopped
2 oz (55g) nibbed almonds	½ cupful nibbed almonds
Finely grated zest of 1 orange	Finely grated zest of 1 orange
2 teaspoonsful clear honey	2 teaspoonsful clear honey
¼ pint (140ml) soured cream	⅔ cupful soured cream
Lightly beaten egg white, to glaze	Lightly beaten egg white, to glaze
Decoration:	*Decoration:*
Split blanched almonds, lightly toasted	Split blanched almonds, lightly toasted
Clear honey	Clear honey

1. Combine the wholemeal flour and bicarbonate of soda in a mixing bowl.

2. Rub the margarine into the dry ingredients, using the fingertips, until a breadcrumb consistency is obtained.

3. Fold in the carob powder, raw cane sugar, dried pineapple and almonds, then incorporate the grated orange zest and honey.

4. Beat the soured cream until smooth, then add to the flour mixture, blending all the ingredients together well.

5. Press the mixture evenly into a greased Swiss roll tin measuring approximately 9 x 13 inches (23 x 33cm), then brush the mixture all over with lightly beaten egg white, to glaze the surface.

6. Bake at 350°F/180°C (Gas Mark 4) for 25-30 minutes, until firm to the touch. Allow to cool thoroughly in the baking tin, then cut into slices.

7. Decorate each of the slices with some lightly toasted almonds, secured by spreading the underside of the nuts with some clear honey. Store the slices in an airtight container.

BROWNIES I

Cuts into 16 squares

Brownies are a firm children's favourite in the United States, and are just as delicious made with all natural ingredients. Two methods can be used to make brownies: in the first method carob is used in powdered form, whilst in the second method, a carob bar is used to flavour the brownies.

Imperial (Metric)	American
6 oz (170g) polyunsaturated margarine	¾ cupful polyunsaturated margarine
1 oz (30g) carob powder	¼ cupful carob powder
4 oz (115g) light Muscovado sugar	⅔ cupful light Muscovado sugar
2 eggs, lightly beaten	2 eggs, lightly beaten
2 oz (55g) wholemeal flour	½ cupful wholewheat flour
1 teaspoonful baking powder	1 teaspoonful baking powder
2 oz (55g) walnuts or pecans, chopped	½ cupful English walnuts or pecans, chopped

1. Melt 2 oz (55g) of the margarine in a saucepan set over a moderate heat, then stir the carob powder into the melted margarine, blending well. Set the mixture aside to cool.

2. Cream the rest of the margarine and the light Muscovado sugar together until pale and fluffy.

3. Gradually incorporate the beaten eggs, adding a little at a time, then fold in the flour and baking powder, adding alternately with the melted margarine and carob mixture. Finally, fold in the chopped walnuts.

4. Pour the mixture into a greased 8 inch (20cm) square baking tin, smoothing over the top, and bake at 350°F/180°C (Gas Mark 4) for 35-40 minutes, until firm to the touch.

5. Allow to cool thoroughly in the baking tin, then cut into squares. Store the brownies in an airtight container.

BROWNIES II

Cuts into 16 squares

Imperial (Metric)	American
1 x 2½ oz (75 g) carob bar	1 x 2½ ounce carob bar
4 oz (115 g) polyunsaturated margarine	½ cupful polyunsaturated margarine
2 oz (55 g) Vanilla Sugar (page 189)	⅓ cupful Vanilla Sugar (page 189)
2 eggs, lightly beaten	2 eggs, lightly beaten
4 oz (115 g) wholemeal flour	1 cupful wholewheat flour
1 teaspoonful baking powder	1 teaspoonful baking powder
2 oz (55 g) walnuts or pecans, chopped	½ cupful English walnuts or pecans, chopped

1. Break the carob bar into pieces and place in a heat-resistant bowl, with 1 oz (30 g) of the margarine. Set the bowl over a saucepan of gently simmering water, until the carob and margarine are fully melted.

2. Cream the rest of the margarine and Vanilla Sugar together until pale and fluffy.

3. Gradually incorporate the beaten eggs, adding a little at a time, then beat in the melted carob and margarine mixture.

4. Now fold in the flour, baking powder and walnuts, then spoon the mixture into a greased 8 inch (20 cm) square baking tin. Bake at 350°F/180°C (Gas Mark 4) for 35-40 minutes, until firm to the touch.

5. Allow to cool thoroughly in the baking tin, then cut the brownies into squares. Store in an airtight container.

CAROB COATED LEMON BISCUITS

Makes about 30

These tasty lemon biscuits are all the more delicious with their flavour-contrasting carob coating.

Imperial (Metric)
4 oz (115 g) polyunsaturated margarine
4 oz (115 g) raw cane sugar
Finely grated zest of 2 lemons
1 large egg yolk
6 oz (170 g) wholemeal flour
2 oz (55 g) ground almonds
½ teaspoonful baking powder
Lightly beaten egg white, to glaze

American
½ cupful polyunsaturated margarine
⅔ cupful raw cane sugar
Finely grated zest of 2 lemons
1 large egg yolk
1½ cupsful wholewheat flour
½ cupful ground almonds
½ teaspoonful baking powder
Lightly beaten egg white, to glaze

Coating:
Plain Carob Coating (page 183)

Coating:
Plain Carob Coating (page 183)

1. Cream the margarine, raw cane sugar and finely grated lemon zest together until pale and fluffy.

2. Beat the egg yolk into the creamed ingredients, then fold in the flour, ground almonds and baking powder, mixing to a stiff, workable consistency.

3. Turn out onto a lightly floured board and roll out to a thickness of about ¼ inch (6mm). Cut into rounds with a 2 inch (5cm) fluted biscuit cutter, then transfer the biscuits to lightly greased baking sheets.

4. Brush all over the surface of the biscuits with lightly beaten egg white, to glaze, then bake at 350°F/180°C (Gas Mark 4) for about 15 minutes, until golden brown.

5. Allow to cool thoroughly, then spread the carob coating over the underside of the biscuits. Leave the coating to set, then store the biscuits in an airtight container.

CAROB PEANUT COOKIES

Makes about 20

Dark and crunchy carob cookies, topped with peanuts.

Imperial (Metric)	American
4 oz (115 g) polyunsaturated margarine	½ cupful polyunsaturated margarine
2 oz (55 g) raw cane sugar	⅓ cupful raw cane sugar
6 oz (170 g) wholemeal flour	1½ cupsful wholewheat flour
1 oz (30 g) carob powder	¼ cupful carob powder
1 egg white, lightly beaten	1 egg white, lightly beaten
2 oz (55 g) peanuts, coarsely chopped	½ cupful peanuts, coarsely chopped

1. Cream the margarine and raw cane sugar together until light and fluffy.

2. Fold in the flour and carob powder, mixing to a fairly stiff, workable dough.

3. Turn the mixture onto a lightly floured board and roll out to a thickness of about ¼ inch (6mm). Cut into rounds with a 2 inch (5cm) fluted biscuit cutter and place on lightly greased baking sheets.

4. Brush the cookies with the lightly beaten egg white, then press the chopped peanuts on top. Bake at 350°F/180°C (Gas Mark 4) for 12-15 minutes, until the cookies are crisp and the peanuts golden brown. Store in an airtight container when cool.

CAROB NUT COOKIES

Prepare the cookie mixture in the same way as Carob Peanut Cookies and sprinkle with chopped almonds, cashew nuts, walnuts, etc., in place of the peanuts.

CAROB COATED ANIMAL BISCUITS

Makes about 20

Animal-shaped biscuits never fail to please the children – they are especially delicious with their tasty carob coating.

Imperial (Metric)	American
8 oz (225 g) wholemeal flour	2 cupsful wholewheat flour
4 oz (115 g) polyunsaturated margarine	½ cupful polyunsaturated margarine
3 oz (85 g) Vanilla Sugar (page 189)	½ cupful Vanilla Sugar (page 189)
1 egg, lightly beaten	1 egg, lightly beaten
1 tablespoonful natural yogurt or milk	1 tablespoonful natural yogurt or milk
Coating and Decoration:	*Coating and Decoration:*
Plain Carob Coating (page 00)	Plain Carob Coating (page 00)
Small raisins	Small raisins
Small strips of dried apricot or dried pineapple	Small strips of dried apricot or dried pineapple

1. Place the flour in a mixing bowl, then, using the fingertips, rub the margarine into the flour, until a breadcrumb consistency is obtained.

2. Fold in the Vanilla Sugar, then make a well in the centre of the ingredients and pour in the beaten egg. Begin blending the mixture together, adding sufficient natural yogurt or milk to bind to a fairly stiff consistency.

3. Turn out onto a lightly floured board and roll out to a thickness of about ¼ inch (6mm). Cut into shapes, using animal-shaped biscuit cutters. Place the biscuits on lightly greased baking sheets, then bake at 350°F/180°C (Gas Mark 4) for about 15 minutes, until golden brown.

4. Allow the biscuits to cool, then coat the topside evenly with the melted Carob Coating. Decorate the biscuits with raisins to form the animal eyes and small strips of dried apricot or pineapple to form the mouths. Store the biscuits in an airtight container when the Carob Coating has set.

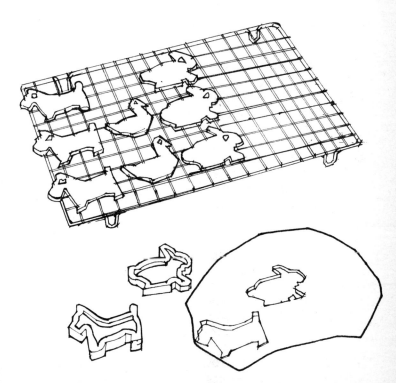

CAROB ROLLED OAT SLICES

Cuts into 10-12 slices

Imperial (Metric)	American
4 oz (115 g) block carob	4 ounce block carob
4 oz (115 g) polyunsaturated margarine	½ cupful polyunsaturated margarine
1 tablespoonful clear honey	1 tablespoonful clear honey
8 oz (225 g) rolled oats	2 cupful rolled oats
2 oz (55 g) desiccated coconut	¾ cupful desiccated coconut

1. Break the carob into pieces and place in a saucepan with the margarine and honey. Set the saucepan over a low heat, until all the ingredients are fully melted.

2. Remove from the heat and stir in the rolled oats and coconut, mixing well.

3. Spread the mixture evenly into a greased shallow baking tin and bake at 350°F/180°C (Gas Mark 4) for 20-25 minutes.

4. Allow to cool slightly in the baking tin, then mark into slices. Remove the slices from the baking tin when completely cooled, then store in an airtight container.

5.
ICES AND ICED DESSERTS

Combined with vanilla, orange and coffee, carob makes a particularly delicious ice cream flavourant. Sprinkled with nuts, coated with an accompanying cream sauce or moulded into the shape of a cake, these carob-flavoured ice creams will never fail to please. Use the ices to prepare desserts such as a Calypso Sundae or a Banana Split, or for a more elaborate creation, serve a whole fresh pineapple filled with alternating layers of carob and orange flavoured ice cream and the juicy fresh pineapple flesh.

CAROB ICE CREAM

Serves 4-6

A velvety smooth and creamy ice, rich in the combined flavours of carob and vanilla.

Imperial (Metric)	American
¾ pint (425 ml) single cream	2 cupsful light cream
1 vanilla pod, split lengthways	1 vanilla bean, split lengthways
4 egg yolks	4 egg yolks
3 oz (85 g) light Muscovado sugar	½ cupful light Muscovado sugar
1 x 2½ oz (75 g) carob bar	1 x 2½ ounce carob bar
¼ pint (140 ml) double cream	⅔ cupful heavy cream

1. Reserve 3 tablespoonsful of the single cream, then place the remainder in a saucepan with the vanilla pod and heat to boiling point. Cover and set aside to infuse for about 15 minutes, so that the flavour of the vanilla pod penetrates the cream. Remove the vanilla pod after the infusion time, then re-heat the cream to simmering point.

2. Whisk the egg yolks and Muscovado sugar together until the mixture lightens and becomes thick and creamy.

3. Gradually pour the infused cream onto the egg mixture, in a thin stream, stirring constantly as the eggs are slowly warmed by the hot cream. Pour the mixture into a heavy-based saucepan and allow to thicken very gradually, over a gentle heat, without allowing to boil. Stir the mixture constantly with a wooden spoon and remove from the heat when it has thickened sufficiently to coat the back of the spoon. (The thickening process will take about 10 minutes and the mixture must not be allowed to come anywhere near to boiling point, or else

it will curdle.) Strain the custard into a clean bowl.

4. Meanwhile, break the carob bar into pieces and place in a heat-resistant bowl, with the reserved 3 tablespoonsful of single cream. Set the bowl over a saucepan of gently simmering water until the carob and cream are melted to a smooth paste. Stir the melted carob mixture into the vanilla-flavoured custard, blending well, then set the mixture aside to cool.

5. Whip the double cream until it stands in soft peaks, then fold into the cooled carob and vanilla custard, blending well. Pour into a freezing container and freeze for about 1 hour until the mixture has begun to thicken and is partially iced. Remove from the freezer and beat well to break up the ice crystals, then return to the freezer. Remove and beat again several more times at 30 minute intervals, then freeze until firm. Allow the ice cream to soften slightly in the refrigerator before serving.

MOCHA ICE CREAM

Serves 4-6

The combined flavours of carob, coffee and vanilla give an exceptionally delicious and flavour-rich ice cream.

Imperial (Metric)	American
¾ pint (425 ml) milk	2 cupsful milk
1 vanilla pod, split lengthways	1 vanilla bean, split lengthways
2 tablespoonsful decaffeinated coffee	2 tablespoonsful decaffeinated coffee
3 fl oz (90 ml) boiling water	⅓ cupful boiling water
1 x 2½ oz (75 g) carob bar	1 x 2½ ounce carob bar
4 egg yolks	4 egg yolks
3 oz (85 g) light Muscovado sugar	½ cupful light Muscovado sugar
¼ pint (140 ml) double cream	⅔ cupful heavy cream

1. Heat the milk and vanilla pod to boiling point, then cover and set aside to infuse for about 15 minutes.

2. Make a concentrated coffee by dissolving the decaffeinated coffee in the boiling water.

3. Break the carob bar into small pieces and place in a heat-resistant bowl, together with the concentrated coffee. Set the bowl over a saucepan of gently simmering water, to melt the carob. Blend the melted carob and coffee together until smooth and glossy.

4. Meanwhile, whisk the egg yolks and Muscovado sugar together until the mixture lightens and becomes thick and creamy.

5. Remove the vanilla pod from the milk after the infusion time, then re-heat the milk to simmering point. Now slowly pour the hot, vanilla-flavoured milk onto the

egg mixture, in a thin stream, stirring constantly. Pour the mixture into a heavy-based saucepan and allow to thicken very gradually, over a gentle heat, without allowing to boil. Stir the mixture continuously with a wooden spoon and remove from the heat when it has thickened sufficiently to coat the back of the spoon. (This will take about 10 minutes.)

6. Strain the vanilla custard into a clean bowl, then stir in the blended carob and coffee concentrate, mixing well. Leave the mocha custard to stand in a cool place and allow to cool.

7. Whip the double cream until it stands in soft peaks, then fold into the cooled mocha custard, blending well. Pour into a freezing container and freeze for about 1 hour until partially iced. Remove from the freezer and beat well to break up the ice crystals, then return to the freezer. Remove and beat again several more times at 30 minute intervals, then freeze until firm. Allow the ice cream to soften slightly in the refrigerator before serving.

MOCHA ICE CREAM CAKE

Mocha Ice Cream (or any other flavour) makes an attractive and elegant dessert served in the shape of a cake. This is a simple operation, and the final result is most appealing.

Prepare the Mocha Ice Cream custard by the indicated method. After the final beating of the ice cream in the freezing container, spoon the partially frozen ice into a 7 inch (18cm) round, loose-bottomed cake tin, making sure that the ice cream is firmly packed and the top smooth and even. Cover with foil and freeze until firm.

Shortly before serving, run a knife around the edge of the

cake tin to loosen the sides of the ice cream cake, then gently ease out of the tin and place on a chilled serving plate. Garnish the cake with some carob leaves and a fresh flower. Cut the cake into wedges at the table, using a knife dipped in hot water.

CAROB AND ORANGE ICE CREAM

Serves 4-6

Imperial (Metric)	American
¾ pint (425 ml) single cream	2 cupsful light cream
4 egg yolks	4 egg yolks
3 oz (85 g) light Muscovado sugar	½ cupful light Muscovado sugar
Finely grated zest of 1 orange	Finely grated zest of 1 orange
1 x 2½ oz (75 g) carob bar	1 x 2½ ounce carob bar
Juice of 1 orange	Juice of 1 orange
¼ pint (140 ml) double cream	⅔ cupful heavy cream

1. Place the single cream in a saucepan and heat to boiling point. Remove from the heat and set aside to cool slightly.

2. Whisk the egg yolks and Muscovado sugar together until the mixture lightens and becomes thick and creamy.

3. Gradually pour the hot cream onto the egg mixture, in a thin stream, stirring constantly as the eggs are slowly warmed by the hot liquid. Pour into a heavy-based saucepan and allow to thicken very gradually, over a gentle heat, without allowing to boil. Stir the mixture constantly with a wooden spoon and remove from the heat when it has thickened sufficiently to coat the back of the spoon. (This will take about 10 minutes.)

4. Strain the custard into a clean bowl, then stir in the finely grated orange zest.

5. Break the carob bar into pieces and place in a heat-resistant bowl with the orange juice. Set the bowl over a saucepan of gently simmering water, until the carob and orange juice are blended to a smooth paste. Add the carob and orange mixture to the prepared custard, blending thoroughly, then set the custard aside until completely cool.

6. Whip the double cream until it stands in soft peaks, then fold into the cooled carob and orange custard, blending well. Pour into a freezing container and freeze for about 1 hour until the mixture has begun to thicken and is partially iced. Remove from the freezer and beat well to break up the ice crystals, then return to the freezer. Remove and beat again several more times at 30 minute intervals, then freeze until firm. Allow the ice cream to soften slightly in the refrigerator before serving.

PEARS BELLE HÉLÈNE

Serves 4

Vanilla-poached pears served with vanilla ice cream, coated with a carob cream sauce and sprinkled with toasted almonds.

Imperial (Metric)	American
4 firm, ripe pears	4 firm, ripe pears
Juice of 1 lemon	Juice of 1 lemon
¾ pint (425 ml) water	2 cupsful water
4 oz (115 g) raw cane sugar	⅔ cupful raw cane sugar
1 vanilla pod, split lengthways	1 vanilla bean, split lengthways

To Serve:	*To Serve:*
4 scoops vanilla ice cream, made with raw cane sugar	4 scoops vanilla ice cream, made with raw cane sugar
Carob and Vanilla Cream Sauce (page 184)	Carob and Vanilla Cream Sauce (page 184)
2 oz (55 g) flaked almonds, lightly toasted	½ cupful slivered almonds, lightly toasted

1. Peel and core the pears, then slice in half lengthways. Brush the pears lightly with lemon juice to prevent them from discolouring.

2. Place the water, raw cane sugar and vanilla pod in a saucepan and bring to the boil, stirring constantly until all the sugar has dissolved. Now lower the heat to simmering point and add the pear halves. Cover with a lid and poach gently for 10-15 minutes, or until the pears are tender but not too soft or in any way disintegrating. Drain the pears out of the cooking juices and set aside to cool.

3. Shortly before serving, place a scoop of vanilla ice cream in individual serving glasses and place a poached pear half at each side of the ice cream. Stand the pear halves upright, then tilt them slightly inwards so that

they touch at the top and cover the vanilla ice.

4. Coat the pears with the Carob and Vanilla Cream Sauce and complete with a sprinkling of lightly toasted flaked almonds.

CALYPSO SUNDAE

Serves 2

A taste of the tropics is contained in this mocha-flavoured ice cream sundae, coated with a Jamaican coffee liqueur.

Imperial (Metric)	American
4 scoops Mocha Ice Cream (page 134)	4 scoops Mocha Ice Cream (page 134)
2 tablespoonsful *Tia Maria*	2 tablespoonsful *Tia Maria*
2 tablespoonsful lightly whipped cream	2 tablespoonsful lightly whipped cream
2 oz (55 g) flaked almonds, lightly toasted	½ cupful slivered almonds, lightly toasted

1. Place two scoops of Mocha Ice Cream in individual sundae glasses and coat with some *Tia Maria*.

2. Pipe a swirl of whipped cream over the mocha ice and top with a liberal sprinkling of lightly toasted flaked almonds.

ICED PINEAPPLE

Serves 6-8

A fresh pineapple filled with alternate layers of Carob and Orange Ice Cream and juicy chunks of pineapple makes a stunning iced dessert.

Imperial (Metric)	American
1 large pineapple	1 large pineapple
One quantity Carob and	One quantity Carob and
Orange Ice Cream	Orange Ice Cream
(page 136)	(page 136)
Decoration:	*Decoration:*
Orange slices	Orange slices
Small fresh flowers	Small fresh flowers

1. Slice the top off the pineapple, leaving the tuft of leaves intact, and reserve. Slice a little off the bottom of the pineapple, so that it stands firmly upright, taking care not to cut too deeply and puncture the flesh.

2. Using a sharp knife, carefully extract the pineapple flesh, leaving a ½ inch (1 cm) thickness of flesh attached to the shell. Dice the pineapple flesh into chunks, discarding the hard centre core.

3. Immediately before serving, fill the pineapple shell with alternate layers of Carob and Orange Ice Cream and pineapple chunks, ending with a layer of pineapple.

4. Serve the pineapple on a large serving platter, surrounded by orange slices and small, brightly coloured fresh flowers. Trim any withered parts from the tuft of leaves, then replace on top of the pineapple.

ICED MOCHA MERINGUE

Serves 6-8

A meringue base, covered with a mocha-flavoured ice cream, dotted with fresh cherries.

Imperial (Metric)	American
Meringue Base:	*Meringue Base:*
3 egg whites	3 egg whites
5 oz (140g) light Muscovado sugar	¾ cupful light Muscovado sugar
Topping and Decoration:	*Topping and Decoration:*
Mocha Ice Cream (page 134)	Mocha Ice Cream (page 134)
8 oz (225g) fresh cherries, unstemmed	2 cupful fresh cherries, unstemmed
Sprigs of leaves	Sprigs of leaves

1. To prepare the meringue base, whisk the egg whites until they stand in stiff peaks. Add half the quantity of Muscovado sugar, then continue whisking until the whites regain their former stiffness. Now carefully fold in the remaining sugar.

2. Draw a 9 inch (23cm) circle on a sheet of non-stick or waxed paper and place on a baking sheet. Spoon the meringue onto the marked circle, spreading evenly with a palette knife. Bake the meringue at 250°F/130°C (Gas Mark ½) for 2-3 hours, until crisp and dry. Carefully peel off the lining paper, then place the meringue circle on a large serving platter.

3. Immediately before serving, place the Mocha Ice Cream, in scoops, on top of the meringue base. Dot the fresh cherries all over the base, amidst the ice cream. Complete by decorating with some sprigs of fresh leaves, arranged in a circle on the serving platter, surrounding the meringue base.

BANANA SPLIT

Serves 4

This popular iced dessert is made with a carob and orange flavoured ice cream, sandwiched between banana halves, coated with pure maple syrup and sprinkled with toasted almonds.

Imperial (Metric)	American
4 bananas	4 bananas
4 scoops Carob and Orange Ice Cream (page 136)	4 scoops Carob and Orange Ice Cream (page 136)
4 tablespoonsful pure maple syrup	4 tablespoonsful pure maple syrup
2 oz (55 g) flaked almonds, lightly toasted	½ cupful slivered almonds, lightly toasted

1. Peel the bananas and slice lengthways in half.

2. Place one or two scoops of Carob and Orange Ice Cream in boat-shaped sundae dishes and sandwich between the banana halves.

3. Coat the ice cream and bananas with some pure maple syrup, then top with a liberal sprinkling of lightly toasted almonds.

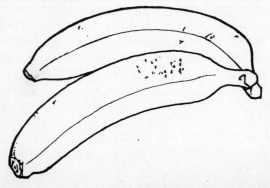

ICED CHOUX RING

Serves 6-8

This unusual iced dessert makes a special treat for the whole family. A tasty wholemeal choux pastry ring is filled with vanilla ice cream, topped with a dark and delicious carob coating and sprinkled with toasted almonds.

Imperial (Metric)	American
One quantity wholemeal choux pastry (page 60)	One quantity wholewheat choux pastry (page 60)
Plain Carob Coating (page 183)	Plain Carob Coating (page 183)
2 oz (55g) flaked almonds, lightly toasted	½ cupful slivered almonds, lightly toasted
1 pint (570ml) vanilla ice cream made with raw cane sugar	2½ cupsful vanilla ice cream, made with raw cane sugar

1. Prepare the Wholemeal Choux Pastry as indicated, then use the pastry to prepare an 8 inch (20cm) ring, using the same preparation and baking method as that given for the Almond Choux Ring (page 60).

2. When cool, split the choux pastry ring in half. Spread the Carob Coating over the top half of the ring, then sprinkle with some lightly toasted flaked almonds. Allow the Carob Coating to set.

3. Place the lower half of the choux pastry ring on a serving platter, then immediately before serving, spoon the vanilla ice cream on top of the pastry. Now replace the carob and almond coated pastry top, covering the ice cream filling. Serve the dessert at once.

6.
HOT PUDDINGS

Hot puddings are traditional, ever-popular family favourites. But as a natural-food minded cook you may feel dubious about incorporating puddings into a healthy eating programme. Prepared with natural, unrefined ingredients they are, however, a warming and nutritious end to a meal on a cold winter's night.

Steamed carob puddings will undoubtedly become a firm favourite with your family. They are full of flavour and goodness and are particularly delicious served with an accompanying vanilla and muscovado custard sauce, or topped with pure maple syrup.

STEAMED CAROB PUDDING

Serves 4-6

Flavoured with carob, vanilla, honey and orange, this is a perfectly delicious family pudding.

Imperial (Metric)	American
4 oz (115 g) polyunsaturated margarine	½ cupful polyunsaturated margarine
2 oz (55 g) Vanilla Sugar (page 189)	⅓ cupful Vanilla Sugar (page 189)
1 tablespoonful clear honey	1 tablespoonful clear honey
Finely grated zest of 1 orange	Finely grated zest of 1 orange
2 eggs, lightly beaten	2 eggs, lightly beaten

5 oz (140g) wholemeal flour	1¼ cupsful wholewheat flour
1 oz (30g) carob powder	¼ cupful carob powder
2 teaspoonsful baking powder	2 teaspoonsful baking powder
1 tablespoonful natural yogurt	1 tablespoonful natural yogurt

To Serve:
2-3 tablespoonsful pure
   maple syrup

To Serve:
2-3 tablespoonsful pure
   maple syrup

1. Cream the margarine, Vanilla Sugar, honey and orange zest together until pale and fluffy.

2. Gradually incorporate the beaten eggs, adding a little at a time.

3. Now fold in the flour, carob powder and baking powder, together with sufficient natural yogurt to give a soft dropping consistency.

4. Spoon the mixture into a greased 1½ pint (850ml) pudding basin, cover with greaseproof paper or foil and secure with string.

5. Steam the pudding for about 1½ hours, until nicely risen and firm to the touch. Serve the pudding piping hot, topped with some pure maple syrup.

CAROB PINEAPPLE UPSIDE-DOWN PUDDING

Serves 6

Imperial (Metric)	American
1 small fresh pineapple	1 small fresh pineapple
2 tablespoonsful clear honey	2 tablespoonsful clear honey
1 oz (30 g) cherries	¼ cupful cherries
4 oz (115 g) polyunsaturated margarine	½ cupful polyunsaturated margarine
3 oz (85 g) raw cane sugar	½ cupful raw cane sugar
2 eggs, lightly beaten	2 eggs, lightly beaten
4 oz (115 g) wholemeal flour	1 cupful wholewheat flour
2 oz (55 g) carob powder	½ cupful carob powder
2 teaspoonsful baking powder	2 teaspoonsful baking powder
2 tablespoonsful natural yogurt or milk	2 tablespoonsful natural yogurt or milk

1. Cut the top and base off the pineapple, then slice into evenly sized rings. Now cut away the outer peel, small brown 'eyes' and centre core.

2. Well-grease an 8 inch (20 cm) round cake tin and spread the clear honey over the base. Arrange the fresh pineapple slices on top of the layer of honey and place a cherry in each centre core cavity.

3. Cream the margarine and sugar together until light and fluffy.

4. Gradually add the beaten eggs, incorporating a little at a time, then fold in the flour, carob powder and baking powder, together with sufficient yogurt or milk to give a soft dropping consistency.

5. Spoon the carob cake mixture over the pineapple rings, spreading evenly, then bake at 350°F/180°C (Gas Mark 4) for 40-45 minutes, until the cake is nicely risen and firm to the touch.

6. Carefully turn the pudding out onto a warmed serving plate and serve at once, whilst piping hot.

CAROB AND ALMOND LAYER PUDDING

Serves 4-6

This delicious honey and vanilla flavoured carob pudding is speckled with layers of flaked almonds.

Imperial (Metric)	American
4 oz (115 g) polyunsaturated margarine	½ cupful polyunsaturated margarine
2 oz (55 g) Vanilla Sugar (page 189)	⅓ cupful Vanilla Sugar (page 189)
2 tablespoonsful clear honey	2 tablespoonsful clear honey
2 eggs, lightly beaten	2 eggs, lightly beaten
5 oz (140 g) wholemeal flour	1¼ cupsful wholewheat flour
1 oz (30 g) carob powder	¼ cupful carob powder
2 teaspoonsful baking powder	2 teaspoonsful baking powder
1 tablespoonful natural yogurt or milk	1 tablespoonful natural yogurt or milk
8 oz (225 g) flaked almonds	2 cupsful slivered almonds

1. Cream the margarine, Vanilla Sugar and 1 tablespoonful of clear honey together until pale and fluffy.

2. Gradually incorporate the beaten eggs, adding a little at a time, then fold in the flour, carob powder and baking powder, adding sufficient natural yogurt or milk to give a soft dropping consistency.

3. Grease a 1½ pint (850 ml) pudding basin and spoon the remaining tablespoonful of clear honey into the bottom of the basin. Sprinkle a layer of flaked almonds over the honey, followed by a layer of the carob pudding mixture. Continue making up alternate layers of flaked almonds and pudding mixture, ending with a final layer of pudding mixture.

4. Cover the basin with greaseproof paper or foil and secure. Steam the pudding for about 1½ hours and serve piping hot.

CAROB CURRANT PUDDING

Serves 4-6

Imperial (Metric)	American
6 oz (170g) wholemeal flour	1½ cupsful wholewheat flour
2 teaspoonsful baking powder	2 teaspoonsful baking powder
4 oz (115g) polyunsaturated margarine	½ cupful polyunsaturated margarine
1 oz (30g) carob powder	¼ cupful carob powder
1 oz (30g) ground almonds	¼ cupful ground almonds
1 oz (30g) light Muscovado sugar	2 tablespoonsful light Muscovado sugar
2 teaspoonsful ground cinnamon	2 teaspoonsful ground cinnamon
6 oz (170g) currants	1 cupful currants
1 egg, lightly beaten	1 egg, lightly beaten
2 tablespoonsful clear honey	2 tablespoonsful clear honey
2 tablespoonsful natural yogurt or milk	2 tablespoonsful natural yogurt or milk

1. Combine the flour and baking powder in a mixing bowl.

2. Rub the margarine into the flour until a breadcrumb consistency is obtained.

3. Fold in the carob powder, ground almonds, Muscovado sugar, cinnamon and currants.

4. Make a well in the centre of the dry ingredients and pour in the egg and honey. Begin blending the ingredients together, adding sufficient yogurt or milk to give a soft dropping consistency.

5. Spoon the mixture into a greased 1½ pint (850ml) pudding basin, then cover with greaseproof paper or foil and secure.

6. Steam the pudding for about 1½ hours, until nicely risen and firm to the touch. Serve whilst piping hot.

CAROB AND PINEAPPLE PUDDINGS

Serves 6

Natural dried pineapple and honey give a specially delicious flavour to these individual carob puddings.

Imperial (Metric)	American
6 teaspoonsful clear honey	6 teaspoonsful clear honey
6 oz (170g) dried pineapple	1 cupful dried pineapple
3 oz (85g) polyunsaturated margarine	⅓ cupful polyunsaturated margarine
2 oz (55g) raw cane sugar	⅓ cupful raw cane sugar
Finely grated zest of 1 orange	Finely grated zest of 1 orange
1 egg, lightly beaten	1 egg, lightly beaten
3 oz (85g) wholemeal flour	¾ cupful wholewheat flour
1 oz (30g) carob powder	¼ cupful carob powder
1½ teaspoonsful baking powder	1½ teaspoonsful baking powder
1-2 tablespoonsful natural yogurt or milk	1-2 tablespoonsful natural yogurt or milk

1. Place one teaspoonful of clear honey into the bottom of six well-greased, large dariole moulds.

2. Dice the dried pineapple into small pieces and place a layer of the pineapple in the bottom of the moulds, covering the honey. Reserve the remaining diced pineapple to add to the sponge mixture.

3. Cream the margarine, raw cane sugar and grated orange zest together until pale and fluffy.

4. Gradually add the beaten egg, incorporating a little at a time, then fold in the flour, carob powder and baking powder.

5. Add the reserved diced pineapple to the sponge mixture, together with sufficient natural yogurt or milk to give a soft dropping consistency.

6. Spoon the mixture into the prepared moulds, cover with greaseproof paper or foil and secure with string.

7. Steam the puddings for about 1 hour, until nicely risen and firm to the touch. Turn out onto individual serving plates and serve piping hot.

CAROB AND APPLE PUDDING

Serves 6

A honey and apple base is covered with a carob-flavoured sponge mixture to make this flavourful baked fruit pudding.

Imperial (Metric)	American
1 lb (455 g) cooking apples	1 lb cooking apples
Finely grated zest of 1 lemon	Finely grated zest of 1 lemon
3 tablespoonsful clear honey	3 tablespoonsful clear honey
3 oz (85 g) polyunsaturated margarine	⅓ cupful polyunsaturated margarine
2 oz (55 g) raw cane sugar	⅓ cupful raw cane sugar
1 egg, lightly beaten	1 egg, lightly beaten
4 oz (115 g) wholemeal flour	1 cupful wholewheat flour
1 oz (30 g) carob powder	¼ cupful carob powder
2 teaspoonsful baking powder	2 teaspoonsful baking powder
2 tablespoonsful natural yogurt or milk	2 tablespoonsful natural yogurt or milk

1. Peel and core the apples, then slice the fruit into a well greased 1½ pint (850 ml) ovenproof pudding dish. Finely grate the lemon zest onto the apples, then spoon the honey over the fruit.

2. Cream the margarine and raw cane sugar together until light and fluffy.

3. Gradually incorporate the beaten egg, adding a little at a time.

4. Fold in the flour, carob powder and baking powder, together with sufficient natural yogurt or milk to give a soft dropping consistency.

5. Spoon the carob mixture over the apples and honey, spreading evenly, then bake at 350°F/180°C (Gas Mark

4) for 40-45 minutes, until nicely risen and firm to the touch. Serve the pudding piping hot.

CAROB BUTTERMILK PUDDING

Serves 6

Imperial (Metric)	American
4 oz (115 g) polyunsaturated margarine	½ cupful polyunsaturated margarine
2 oz (55 g) raw cane sugar	⅓ cupful raw cane sugar
1 tablespoonful clear honey	1 tablespoonful clear honey
Finely grated zest of 1 orange	Finely grated zest of 1 orange
1 egg, lightly beaten	1 egg, lightly beaten
5 oz (140 g) wholemeal flour	1¼ cupsful wholewheat flour
2 oz (55 g) carob powder	½ cupful carob powder
2 teaspoonsful baking powder	2 teaspoonsful baking powder
2-3 tablespoonsful buttermilk	2-3 tablespoonsful buttermilk

1. Cream the margarine, raw cane sugar, honey and finely grated orange zest together until pale and fluffy.

2. Gradually incorporate the beaten egg, adding a little at a time.

3. Fold in the flour, carob powder and baking powder, together with sufficient buttermilk to give a soft dropping consistency.

4. Spoon the mixture into a greased 1½ pint (850ml) pudding basin, then cover with greaseproof paper or foil and secure.

5. Steam the pudding for 1½-2 hours, until nicely risen and firm to the touch. Serve piping hot.

STEAMED CAROB BREAD PUDDING

Serves 6

This unusual pudding is made with wholemeal breadcrumbs in place of wholemeal flour and is flavoured with carob, vanilla and orange.

Imperial (Metric)
1 x 2½oz (75g) carob bar
2oz (55g) polyunsaturated margarine
¼ pint (140ml) milk
2oz (55g) Vanilla Sugar (page 189)
2 large eggs, separated
5oz (140g) fresh wholemeal breadcrumbs
Finely grated zest of 1 orange

To Serve:
2-3 tablespoonsful pure maple syrup

American
1 x 2½ ounce carob bar
¼ cupful polyunsaturated margarine
⅔ cupful milk
⅓ cupful Vanilla Sugar (page 189)
2 large eggs, separated
2½ cupsful fresh wholewheat breadcrumbs
Finely grated zest of 1 orange

To Serve:
2-3 tablespoonsful pure maple syrup

1. Break the carob bar into small pieces and place in a saucepan with the margarine. Set the saucepan over a gentle heat until the carob and margarine are fully melted, then blend the milk into the melted ingredients.

2. Away from the heat, stir in the Vanilla Sugar, egg yolks, wholemeal breadcrumbs and grated orange zest, blending all the ingredients together well.

3. In a separate bowl, whisk the egg whites until they stand in stiff peaks, then carefully fold into the carob and breadcrumb mixture, incorporating as lightly as possible so that the whites retain as much of their volume as possible.

4. Spoon the mixture into a well-greased 1½ pint/850 ml pudding basin, then cover with greaseproof paper or foil and secure with string.

5. Steam the pudding for about 1½ hours, until nicely risen and firm to the touch.

6. Turn the pudding out onto a warmed serving plate and serve piping hot, topped with some pure maple syrup.

CAROB AND ORANGE LAYER PUDDINGS

Serves 6

Alternate layers of carob and orange flavoured sponge are contained in these tasty steamed puddings.

Imperial (Metric)	American
4 oz (115 g) polyunsaturated margarine	½ cupful polyunsaturated margarine
4 oz (115 g) raw cane sugar	⅔ cupful raw cane sugar
2 eggs, lightly beaten	2 eggs, lightly beaten
5 oz (140 g) wholemeal flour	1¼ cupsful wholewheat flour
2 teaspoonsful baking powder	2 teaspoonsful baking powder
1 tablespoonful natural yogurt or milk	1 tablespoonful natural yogurt or milk
1 oz (30 g) carob powder	¼ cupful carob powder
Finely grated zest of 1 orange	Finely grated zest of 1 orange
2 teaspoonsful pure orange juice	2 teaspoonsful pure orange juice
6 teaspoonsful raw cane sugar marmalade	6 teaspoonsful raw cane sugar marmalade

1. Cream the margarine and raw cane sugar together until light and fluffy.

2. Gradually add the beaten eggs, incorporating a little at a time, then fold in the flour, baking powder and yogurt or milk.

3. Now divide the mixture into two equal parts. Add the carob powder to one half of the mixture and the grated orange zest and orange juice to the remaining half.

4. Put a teaspoonful of marmalade into the bottom of 6 well-greased large dariole moulds. Spoon alternate layers of the carob and orange flavoured mixtures into the dariole moulds, allowing room for the puddings to rise whilst steaming.

5. Cover the moulds with greaseproof paper or foil and secure. Steam for about 1 hour, until nicely risen and firm to the touch. Serve the puddings piping hot.

CAROB AND ORANGE BROWN RICE PUDDING

Serves 4-6

This creamy and nutritious brown rice pudding is flavoured with honey, orange zest and a grated carob bar.

Imperial (Metric)	American
2 oz (55 g) short grain brown rice	¼ cupful short grain brown rice
1 pint (570 ml) milk	2½ cupsful milk
3 tablespoonsful clear honey	3 tablespoonsful clear honey
Finely grated zest of 1 orange	Finely grated zest of 1 orange
1 x 2½ oz (75 g) carob bar, grated	1 x 2½ ounce carob bar, grated

1. Rinse the brown rice in a colander and drain thoroughly.

2. Place the rice in a 1½ pint (850 ml) pudding dish, lightly greased with polyunsaturated margarine, and pour the milk on top.

3. Stir in the honey, making sure that it is thoroughly absorbed, then cook at 300°F/150°C (Gas Mark 2) for 2-3 hours, or until the rice is soft and tender.

4. When the pudding has been in the oven for about 1 hour, and the rice has swelled up and thickened, stir in the grated orange zest and grated carob bar, then return to the oven for the remaining cooking time.

CAROB FIG PUDDING

Serves 4-6

Imperial (Metric)	American
6 oz (170g) dried figs (soaked overnight in water)	1¼ cupsful dried figs (soaked overnight in water)
3 oz (85g) polyunsaturated margarine	⅓ cupful polyunsaturated margarine
2 oz (55g) raw cane sugar	⅓ cupful raw cane sugar
Finely grated zest of 1 lemon	Finely grated zest of 1 lemon
2 oz (55g) wholemeal flour	½ cupful wholewheat flour
2 oz (55g) carob powder	½ cupful carob powder
2 oz (55g) fresh wholemeal breadcrumbs	1 cupful fresh wholewheat breadcrumbs
1 oz (30g) ground almonds	¼ cupful ground almonds
1½ teaspoonsful baking powder	1½ teaspoonsful baking powder
1 teaspoonful mixed spice	1 teaspoonful mixed spice
3 tablespoonsful natural yogurt	3 tablespoonsful natural yogurt

To Serve:	*To Serve:*
2-3 tablespoonsful pure maple syrup	2-3 tablespoonsful pure maple syrup

1. Drain the figs after the soaking period, then remove the stalks and dice into small pieces.

2. Cream the margarine, raw cane sugar and finely grated lemon zest together until pale and fluffy.

3. Fold in the flour, carob powder, wholemeal breadcrumbs, ground almonds, baking powder and mixed spice, together with sufficient natural yogurt to give a soft dropping consistency.

4. Spoon the mixture into a greased 1½ pint (850ml) pudding basin, then cover with greaseproof paper or foil and secure.

5. Steam the pudding for 2-2½ hours and serve piping hot, topped with some pure maple syrup.

7.

AFTER-DINNER DELIGHTS

Here are such delights as Carob Hazelnut Clusters, Carob Coated Almonds, Carob Fruit and Nut Clusters, Carob Petit Fours – traditional, ever-popular favourites made with natural, unrefined ingredients. Think how nice it would be to offer a box of natural ingredient sweets as a gift to a friend or relative, or to offer them to your guests at the end of a dinner party.

Also included in this section are ideas for carob-dipping dried and fresh fruits. Half-coated dried apricots and half-coated chunks of natural dried pineapple make the most attractive and unusual after-dinner delights, whilst a colourful, half-coated fresh strawberry gives unexpectedly delicious results.

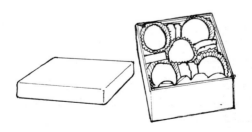

CAROB COATED ALMONDS

Imperial (Metric)
2 x 2½oz (75g) carob bars
6oz (170g) whole blanched
    almonds

American
2 x 2½ ounce carob bars
1½ cupsful whole blanched
    almonds

1. Break the carob bars into small pieces and place in a heat-resistant bowl. Set the bowl over a saucepan of gently simmering water, to melt the carob.

2. Gradually blend a small quantity of water into the melted carob, over the heat, adding a sufficient amount to give a smooth and thick coating consistency.

3. Stir the blanched almonds into the melted carob in small batches, making sure that the nuts are fully coated with the carob.

4. Lay the nuts individually on a sheet of waxed paper and leave to set. Serve the coated nuts in small fluted paper cases, placing two almonds in each paper case.

Variation: Carob makes a delicious combination with all varieties of nuts. As an alternative, try coating whole Brazil nuts, cashew nuts, pecans, or any of your family's favourite nuts, following the same method as above.

HAZELNUT CLUSTERS

Imperial (Metric)
2 x 2½oz (75g) carob bars
6oz (170g) whole hazelnuts,
    roasted and skinned

American
2 x 2½ ounce carob bars
1½ cupsful whole hazelnuts,
    roasted and skinned

1. Melt the carob in a heat-resistant bowl set over a saucepan of gently simmering water. When the carob

has melted, blend in a small amount of water, over the heat, to obtain a smooth and thick coating consistency.

2. Stir the hazelnuts into the melted carob, in small batches, fully coating the nuts.

3. Take a cluster of three coated hazelnuts and place neatly together on a sheet of waxed paper.

4. Leave the clusters to set, then serve in small fluted paper cases.

Variation: Prepare the nut clusters with roasted peanuts or lightly toasted nibbed almonds in place of the hazelnuts.

FRUIT AND NUT CLUSTERS

Imperial (Metric)	American
2 x 2½oz (75g) carob bars	2 x 2½oz carob bars
3oz (85g) nibbed almonds, lightly toasted	¾ cupful nibbed almonds, lightly toasted
3oz (85g) small raisins	½ cupful small raisins

1. Break the carob bars into small pieces and place in a heat-resistant bowl. Set the bowl over a saucepan of gently simmering water, to melt the carob.

2. Gradually blend a little water into the melted carob, over the heat, adding a sufficient amount to give a smooth and thick coating consistency.

3. Mix the almonds and raisins together, then stir into the melted carob, in small batches.

4. When fully coated, spoon small clusters of the fruit and nuts onto waxed paper and leave to set. Serve the clusters in small fluted paper cases.

ALMOND TRUFFLES

Imperial (Metric)	American
4 oz (115 g) wholemeal sponge cake	4 ounces wholewheat sponge cake
4 oz (115 g) ground almonds	1 cupful ground almonds
Clear honey or pure maple syrup	Clear honey or pure maple syrup
Sherry	Sherry
Carob powder	Carob powder

1. Break the wholemeal sponge cake into crumbs and mix with the ground almonds.

2. Add sufficient clear honey/maple syrup and sherry to bind the mixture to a fairly stiff dough.

3. Take small portions of the mixture and roll into small balls between the palms of the hands.

4. Toss in carob powder, coating thoroughly, and serve the truffles in small fluted paper cases.

FRUIT AND NUT TRUFFLES

Imperial (Metric)	American
4 oz (115 g) wholemeal sponge cake	4 ounces wholewheat sponge cake
2 oz (55 g) blanched almonds, finely chopped	½ cupful blanched almonds, finely chopped
2 oz (55 g) small raisins, finely chopped	⅓ cupful small raisins, finely chopped
Clear honey or pure maple syrup	Clear honey or pure maple syrup
Sherry	Sherry
Carob powder	Carob powder

1. Break the wholemeal sponge cake into crumbs and combine with the finely chopped almonds and raisins.

2. Add sufficient clear honey/maple syrup and sherry to bind the ingredients to a stiff dough.

3. Take portions of the mixture and mould into small balls between the palms of the hands

4. Toss the truffles in carob powder, fully coating, and serve in small fluted paper cases.

CAROB DIPPED PINEAPPLE

Imperial (Metric)	American
1 x 2½oz (75g) carob bar	1 x 2½ ounce carob bar
6oz (170g) dried pineapple chunks	1¼ cupsful dried pineapple chunks

1. Break the carob bar into pieces and place in a heat-resistant bowl. Set the bowl over a saucepan of gently simmering water, to melt the carob. Gradually blend some water into the melted carob, over the heat, adding a sufficient amount to obtain a smooth and thick coating consistency.

2. Using a small dipping fork, dip the pineapple chunks into the melted carob, immersing just the bottom half of the chunks, so that the fruit is half-coated with the carob.

3. **Allow the excess carob to drip off, then lay the pineapple chunks on a sheet of waxed paper and leave to set. Serve the coated pineapple in small paper cases.**

CAROB DIPPED APRICOTS

Choose plump and tender dried apricots, with a good colour, for carob dipping.

Following the same method as on the previous page, dip the bottom half of the dried apricots into melted carob, half-coating the fruit, then leave to set on waxed paper. Serve in small fluted paper cases.

CAROB DIPPED STRAWBERRIES

Choose firm fresh strawberries, with the stalks intact, for carob dipping.

First rinse the fruit in a colander, then dry very thoroughly, patting with absorbent paper. Hold the strawberries by the stalks, then dip into melted carob, so that the fruit is half-coated with the carob.

Lay the fruit on waxed paper to set, then serve in small fluted paper cases.

CHERRY CUPS

Imperial (Metric)	American
2 x 2½ oz (75g) carob bars	2 x 2½ ounce carob bars
Small piece wholemeal sponge cake	Small piece wholewheat sponge cake
Sherry	Sherry
Morello or Maraschino cherries, halved	Morello or Maraschino cherries, halved

1. Break one of the carob bars into pieces and place in a heat-resistant bowl. Set the bowl over a saucepan of gently simmering water, to melt the carob. When melted, add a small quantity of water to the carob in order to obtain a smooth and thick coating consistency.

2. Place two small fluted paper cases together (one inside the other) and place a small amount of melted carob in the bottom. Swirl the melted carob around the case, making sure that the sides and bottom are fully coated. Leave to set.

3. Break a small piece of wholemeal sponge cake into crumbs and soak in a little sherry. Place small amounts of the cake and sherry mixture in the bottom of each of the moulded carob cups, then top with half a morello or maraschino cherry.

4. Melt the remaining carob bar over hot water, obtaining the correct coating consistency as above, then spoon on top of the cherries, making sure that the cups are completely sealed. Allow to set thoroughly before serving.

CAROB MARZIPAN SQUARES

Imperial (Metric)	American
8 oz (225 g) ground almonds	2 cupsful ground almonds
1 egg, lightly beaten	1 egg, lightly beaten
1 tablespoonful clear honey	1 tablespoonful clear honey
1 x 2½ oz (75 g) carob bar	1 x 2½ ounce carob bar

1. Mix the ground almonds, egg and honey together, kneading to a smooth and soft dough.

2. Roll the marzipan out to about ½ inch (1 cm) in thickness, then cut into evenly sized squares. Set aside in a warm, dry place for about 1 hour.

3. Break the carob bar into pieces and place in a heat-resistant bowl. Set the bowl over a saucepan of gently simmering water, to melt the carob.

4. Gradually blend some water into the melted carob, adding a sufficient amount to give a smooth and thick coating consistency.

5. Dip the marzipan squares into the melted carob, then place on waxed paper and leave to set. Serve in small fluted paper cases.

CAROB AND ALMOND MARZIPAN DIAMONDS

Make the honey-sweetened marzipan as indicated above, then roll out and cut into diamond shapes. Press a whole almond on top of each marzipan diamond, then set aside to dry for about 1 hour. Coat with melted carob and serve in small fluted paper cases when set.

CAROB CHERRY DREAMS

Fresh cherries are encased in a honey and almond marzipan and covered with a dark and glossy carob coating – a perfectly delectable after-dinner delight.

Imperial (Metric)	American
8 oz (225 g) ground almonds	2 cupsful ground almonds
1 egg, lightly beaten	1 egg, lightly beaten
1 tablespoonful clear honey	1 tablespoonful clear honey
8 oz (225 g) firm fresh cherries, unstemmed	2 cupsful firm fresh cherries, unstemmed
1 x 2½ oz (75 g) carob bar	1 x 2½ ounce carob bar

1. Mix the ground almonds, beaten egg and honey together, blending to a smooth and soft, workable dough.

2. Roll the marzipan out fairly thinly, then take small pieces and wrap around the cherries, leaving the stems intact. Mould the marzipan around the fruit with the hands so that the casing is smooth and neat. Set aside in a warm, dry place for about 1 hour.

3. Break the carob bar into pieces and place in a heat-resistant bowl. Set the bowl over a saucepan of gently simmering water, to melt the carob.

4. Gradually blend some water into the melted carob, over the heat, adding a sufficient amount to give a smooth and thick coating consistency. Hold the cherries by the stems and dip into the melted carob, then place on waxed paper to set. Serve in small fluted **paper cases and eat within 24 hours.**

CAROB PETITS FOURS

To make these attractive petits fours, small pieces of orange-flavoured wholemeal sponge are coated with an almond marzipan and masked in melted carob.

Imperial (Metric)	American
6 oz (170g) polyunsaturated margarine	¾ cupful polyunsaturated margarine
6 oz (170g) raw cane sugar	1 cupful raw cane sugar
Finely grated zest of 1 orange	Finely grated zest of 1 orange
3 eggs, lightly beaten	3 eggs, lightly beaten
6 oz (170g) wholemeal flour	1½ cupsful wholewheat flour
2 teaspoonsful baking powder	2 teaspoonsful baking powder
1 tablespoonful natural yogurt or milk	1 tablespoonful natural yogurt or milk

Almond Marzipan:
8 oz (225g) ground almonds	2 cupsful ground almonds
1 egg, lightly beaten	1 egg, lightly beaten
1 tablespoonful clear honey	1 tablespoonful clear honey

Coating and Decoration:
2 x 2½ oz (75g) carob bars	2 x 2½ ounce carob bars
Split blanched almonds	Split blanched almonds
Small pieces of dried pineapple or dried apricot	Small pieces of dried pineapple or dried apricot
Clear honey	Clear honey

1. Cream the margarine, raw cane sugar and finely grated orange zest together until light and fluffy.

2. Gradually add the beaten eggs, incorporating a little at a time, then fold in the flour and baking powder, adding the yogurt or milk to give a soft dropping consistency.

3. Spoon the mixture into a Swiss roll tin measuring approximately 9 x 13 inches (23 x 33cm), and lined with greased greaseproof paper.

4. Spread the mixture evenly with a palette knife, then bake at 375°F/190°C (Gas Mark 5) for about 15 minutes, until firm to the touch.

5. Allow the cake to cool thoroughly, then cut into diamond, heart, triangle, circle shapes etc., using small petits fours cutters.

6. To make the almond marzipan, mix the ground almonds, beaten egg and honey together, to form a soft dough. Roll out thinly, then cut the marzipan into the same shapes as the wholemeal sponge, using the petits fours cutters. Now coat the sponge shapes with clear honey, then cover with the appropriate marzipan shapes.

7. Break the carob bars into small pieces and place in a heat-resistant bowl. Set the bowl over a saucepan of gently simmering water, to melt the carob. Gradually blend a small quantity of water into the melted carob, over the heat, adding a sufficient amount to give a smooth and thick coating consistency.

8. Lay the petits fours on wire racks, then spoon the carob coating on top. Before the coating sets, decorate the petits fours with some split blanched almonds or small pieces of dried pineapple or dried apricot. Allow the carob coating to set completely, then serve the petits fours in small fluted paper cases.

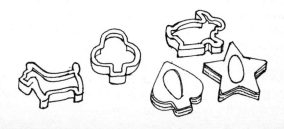

CAROB COATED STUFFED DATES

Imperial (Metric)
1 x 2½oz (75g) carob bar
12 whole dates
12 blanched almonds

American
1 x 2½ ounce carob bar
12 whole dates
12 blanched almonds

1. Stone the dates and stuff each one with a whole blanched almond, pressing the joints firmly together.

2. Break the carob bar into small pieces and place in a heat-resistant bowl set over a saucepan of gently simmering water. When the carob has melted, add a small amount of water to it, to obtain a smooth and thick coating consistency.

3. Using a small dipping fork, dip the stuffed dates into the melted carob, fully coating, then lay the coated dates on a sheet of waxed paper and leave to set. Serve in small fluted paper cases.

8.

DRINKS

Long, cool summer drinks and hot, warming winter night-caps – delicious and nutritious for children and adults alike. Made with natural, additive-free ingredients, they are the perfect in-between-meal-filler and a nourishing dietary accompaniment for children, particularly those with poor appetites who eat little solid food at regular meal times.

Milk, natural yogurt, honey, carob and fresh fruits are the nutritive, vitamin-packed foods that are the basis of the following hot and cold drinks.

CAROB MILK SHAKE

Serves 2

A delicious and nutritious carob drink, with the protein and goodness of milk, natural yogurt and honey.

Imperial (Metric)	American
½ pint (285 ml) milk, chilled	1⅓ cupsful milk, chilled
2 tablespoonsful natural yogurt, chilled	2 tablespoonsful natural yogurt, chilled
2 teaspoonsful clear honey	2 teaspoonsful clear honey
1 tablespoonful carob powder	1 tablespoonful carob powder

To Serve:	*To serve:*
Grated block carob	Grated block carob

1. Place the milk, natural yogurt, honey and carob powder in an electric blender and blend at high speed until the milk shake is smooth, with a frothy head on top.

2. Pour into tall glasses and sprinkle with some grated carob. Serve at once, whilst nice and cool.

CAROB BANANA COOLER

Serves 2

A cooling blend of milk, banana, natural yogurt and honey, topped with a carob and orange-flavoured ice cream.

Imperial (Metric)	American
1 banana	1 banana
½ pint (285 ml) milk, chilled	1⅓ cupsful milk, chilled
2 tablespoonsful natural yogurt, chilled	2 tablespoonsful natural yogurt, chilled
2 teaspoonsful clear honey	2 teaspoonsful clear honey

2 scoops Carob and Orange
Ice Cream (page 136)

2 scoops Carob and Orange
Ice Cream (page 136)

1. Peel the banana and slice into an electric blender. Add
the milk, natural yogurt and honey, then blend until
completely smooth.

2. Pour into tall glasses and top with a scoop of Carob and
Orange Ice Cream. Serve at once.

CAROB NIGHT-CAP

Serves 2

A soothing and nourishing bed-time drink.

Imperial (Metric)	American
¾ pint (425 ml) milk	2 cupsful milk
1 vanilla pod, split lengthways	1 vanilla bean, split lengthways
1 tablespoonful carob powder	1 tablespoonful carob powder
2 teaspoonsful clear honey	2 teaspoonsful clear honey
Grated block carob	Grated block carob

1. Place the milk and vanilla pod in a saucepan and heat to
boiling point. Cover and set aside to infuse for about 10
minutes, so that the flavour of the vanilla pod penetrates
the milk.

2. Remove the vanilla pod after the infusion time, then
pour the warm milk into an electric blender, together
with the carob powder and honey. Blend at high speed
until smooth and foaming.

3. Return to the saucepan and heat the drink to boiling
point. Serve the night-cap in beakers, sprinkled with
some grated block carob.

SPICED CAROB WARMER

Serves 2

Imperial (Metric)	American
1 x 2½oz (75g) carob bar	1 x 2½ ounce carob bar
¾ pint (425 ml) milk	2 cupsful milk
2 teaspoonsful honey or raw cane sugar	2 teaspoonsful honey or raw cane sugar
¼ teaspoonful ground nutmeg	¼ teaspoonful ground nutmeg
½ teaspoonful ground cinnamon	½ teaspoonful ground cinnamon
To serve:	*To serve:*
2 long cinnamon sticks	2 long cinnamon sticks

1. Break the carob bar into pieces, reserving one small piece for grating on top of the drink. Place the remainder in a heat-resistant bowl and set over a saucepan of gently simmering water, to melt.

2. Warm the milk in a saucepan, then incorporate the melted carob, honey and spices. Pour into an electric blender and blend at high speed until smooth and foaming.

3. Return the carob drink to the saucepan and heat to boiling point. Pour into beakers and grate the reserved piece of carob on top of the drink.

4. Place a cinnamon stick in each beaker, to be used as a stirrer in place of a spoon. Serve at once, whilst piping hot.

CAROB HEALTH DRINK

Serves 2

Flavoured with carob and sweetened with honey, this nourishing drink contains the added goodness of protein-rich brewer's yeast.

Imperial (Metric)	American
¾ pint (425 ml) milk	2 cupsful milk
1 tablespoonful carob powder	1 tablespoonful carob powder
2 teaspoonsful brewer's yeast	2 teaspoonsful brewer's yeast
2 teaspoonsful clear honey	2 teaspoonsful clear honey
Grated block carob	Grated block carob

1. Warm the milk in a saucepan, then pour into an electric blender, together with the carob powder, brewer's yeast and honey. Blend at high speed until smooth and foaming.

2. Return the mixture to the saucepan and heat to boiling point. Serve the drink in beakers, sprinkled with some grated block carob.

CAROB EGG NOG

Serves 2

Imperial (Metric)	American
2 eggs	2 eggs
¾ pint (425 ml) milk	2 cupsful milk
1 tablespoonful carob powder	1 tablespoonful carob powder
2 teaspoonsful honey or raw cane sugar	2 teaspoonsful honey or raw cane sugar
2 measures dark rum or brandy	2 measures dark rum or brandy

1. Break each of the eggs into separate beakers and whisk lightly with a fork.

2. Warm the milk in a saucepan, then pour into an electric blender, adding the carob powder and sweetening. Blend at high speed until smooth and foaming.

3. Return the flavoured milk to the saucepan and heat to boiling point. Very slowly pour onto the beaten eggs, stirring constantly, then stir in the rum or brandy to taste. Serve the egg nog at once, whilst piping hot.

9.

CAKE FILLINGS, TOPPINGS AND SAUCES

VANILLA CUSTARD FILLING

This creamy milk and egg based vanilla-flavoured custard is delicious used as a filling for cakes and gâteaux. It is a variation of the French crème pâtissière, the pastry cream so beloved of French chefs.

Imperial (Metric)	American
½ pint (285 ml) milk	1⅓ cupsful milk
1 vanilla pod, split lengthways	1 vanilla bean, split lengthways
3 egg yolks	3 egg yolks
2 oz (55 g) Demerara sugar	⅓ cupful Demerara sugar
¾ oz (20 g) cornflour	2 tablespoonsful cornstarch
2 egg whites	2 egg whites

1. Place the milk and vanilla pod in a saucepan and heat to boiling point. Cover and set aside to infuse for about 15 minutes so that the flavour of the vanilla pod penetrates the milk. Remove the vanilla pod after the infusion time and re-heat the milk to simmering point.

2. Whisk the egg yolks and Demerara sugar together for 1-2 minutes, until the mixture lightens and becomes thick and creamy.

3. Sift the cornflour onto the egg mixture and continue whisking until the dry ingredient is thoroughly incorporated.

Continued overleaf

4. Very gradually pour the hot milk onto the egg mixture, in a thin stream, stirring constantly. Pour into a heavy-based saucepan and cook over a moderate heat, stirring all the time, until the mixture thickens to a smooth and creamy custard. It is essential to beat the vanilla custard vigorously, particularly in the later stages, to prevent the formation of any lumps and also to ensure that the custard does not stick to the bottom of the saucepan. When sufficiently thickened, remove the custard from the heat and set aside to cool.

5. Whisk the egg whites until they stand in stiff peaks, then fold into the cooled vanilla custard, blending well. The custard is now ready to be used as a cake and gâteau filling.

ORANGE CUSTARD FILLING

This custard filling is prepared by the same method as that given for the vanilla custard, but is flavoured with freshly grated orange zest and fresh orange juice.

Imperial (Metric)	American
3 egg yolks	3 egg yolks
2 oz (55 g) Demerara sugar	⅓ cupful Demerara sugar
¾ oz (20 g) cornflour	2 tablespoonsful cornstarch
½ pint (285 ml) milk	1⅓ cupsful milk
Finely grated zest of 1 orange, with a fine, bright skin	Finely grated zest of 1 orange, with a fine, bright skin
2 tablespoonsful freshly squeezed orange juice	2 tablespoonsful freshly squeezed orange juice
2 egg whites	2 egg whites

1. Whisk the egg yolks and sugar together for 1-2 minutes, until the mixture lightens and becomes thick and creamy.

2. Sift the cornflour onto the egg mixture and continue whisking until thoroughly incorporated.

3. Heat the milk to simmering point, then very slowly pour onto the egg mixture in a thin stream, stirring constantly. Pour into a heavy-based saucepan and cook over a moderate heat, stirring all the time, until the mixture thickens to a smooth and creamy custard. Beat the custard very vigorously as it begins to thicken, to prevent the formation of any lumps.

4. When sufficiently thickened, remove the custard from the heat and beat in the orange zest and orange juice. Now return briefly to the heat, stirring all the time, until the custard regains its former thickness. Remove from the heat and set aside to cool.

5. Whisk the egg whites until they stand in stiff peaks, then fold into the cooled orange custard. Use the filling as required in cakes and gâteaux.

VANILLA AND ORANGE CUSTARD FILLING

The flavours of vanilla and orange marry well together and both may be incorporated in a custard filling. Follow the method given for the Orange Custard Filling, but first infuse a vanilla pod in the milk. Use the vanilla-flavoured milk to prepare the custard, then beat in the orange zest and orange juice when thickened, as indicated in the recipe.

ORANGE AND PASSION FRUIT CUSTARD FILLING

This most delicious and unusual of custard fillings is flavoured with the fragrant juice of the exotic little passion fruit.

Imperial (Metric)	American
2 passion fruit	2 passion fruit
1 small orange	1 small orange
½ pint (285 ml) milk	1⅓ cupsful milk
3 egg yolks	3 egg yolks
2 oz (55 g) Demerara sugar	⅓ cupful Demerara sugar
¾ oz (20 g) cornflour	2 tablespoonsful cornstarch
2 egg whites	2 egg whites

1. First rinse the shells of the passion fruit under cold water, removing any particles of grime, then wipe dry.

2. Slice the passion fruit in half and scoop out the seedy pulp into a nylon sieve. Press the fragrant juice through the sieve and reserve the black passion fruit seeds.

3. Rinse the orange and wipe dry. Thinly pare the zest from the orange in a long strip, then place the pared zest in a saucepan with the milk, passion fruit seeds and passion fruit shells.

4. Heat the milk to boiling point, then cover and set aside to infuse for about 15 minutes, so that the flavours of the orange and passion fruit penetrate the milk. Strain the milk after the infusion time, then re-heat to simmering point.

5. Meanwhile, extract the juice from the orange and add two tablespoonsful of the fresh juice to the passion fruit juice.

6. Now whisk the egg yolks and Demerara sugar together for 1-2 minutes, until the mixture lightens and becomes thick and creamy.

7. Sift the cornflour onto the egg mixture and continue whisking until the dry ingredient is thoroughly incorporated.

8. Very gradually pour the hot, infused milk onto the egg mixture, in a thin stream, stirring constantly. Pour into a heavy-based saucepan and cook over a moderate heat, stirring all the time, until the mixture thickens to a smooth and creamy custard. It is essential to beat the custard vigorously as it begins to thicken, to prevent the formation of any lumps and also to ensure that it does not stick to the bottom of the saucepan.

9. When sufficiently thickened, remove from the heat and beat in the combined orange and passion fruit juices. Now return briefly to the heat, stirring all the time, until the custard regains its former thickness. Remove from the heat and set aside to cool.

10. Whisk the egg whites until they stand in stiff peaks, then fold into the cooled custard. The custard filling is now ready to be used in cakes and gâteaux; it is particularly delicious served in combination with other exotic fruits such as mangoes, papayas, pineapples and kiwi fruit.

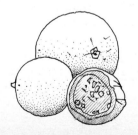

SOURED CREAM FILLING

A smooth and creamy blend, ideal for filling and coating cakes.

Imperial (Metric)	American
1 x 2½ oz (75g) carob bar	1 x 2½ ounce carob bar
¼ pint (140ml) soured cream	⅔ cupful soured cream

1. Break the carob bar into pieces and place in a heat-resistant bowl. Set the bowl over a saucepan of gently simmering water, to melt the carob.

2. Beat the soured cream until smooth, then add to the melted carob over the heat, blending well to a smooth and creamy consistency.

3. Remove from the heat and chill for about 30 minutes. During this time the mixture will thicken to an ideal filling and coating consistency.

ORANGE BUTTER CREAM

Imperial (Metric)	American
2 oz (55g) butter	¼ cupful butter
1 oz (30g) light Muscovado sugar	2 tablespoonsful light Muscovado sugar
Finely grated zest of 1 orange	Finely grated zest of 1 orange
1 teaspoonful freshly squeezed orange juice	1 teaspoonful freshly squeezed orange juice

1. Beat the butter with a wooden spoon until smooth and creamy.

2. Beat the Muscovado sugar into the creamed butter, adding a little at a time, then add the grated orange zest. Lastly beat in the orange juice, adding a drop at a time.

Note: This butter cream is particularly good used as a topping for loaf cakes. It combines especially well with strong flavoured cakes such as spiced or ginger cakes. It also adds a decorative finish to the cake, particularly if the butter cream is topped with some quartered orange slices and/or nuts.

PLAIN CAROB COATING

This plain carob coating is dark, smooth and glossy – a delicious topping for cakes and gâteaux.

Imperial (Metric)	American
1 x 2½oz (75g) carob bar	1 x 2½ ounce carob bar
3-4 floz (90-115ml) water	⅓-½ cupful water

1. Break the carob bar into pieces and place in a heat-resistant bowl. Set the bowl over a saucepan of gently simmering water to melt the carob.

2. When the carob has melted, gradually incorporate the water over the heat, adding a sufficient amount to give a thick and glossy coating. Use the coating at once.

CAROB CREAM COATING

Melt one carob bar over hot water, as above. Gradually blend some double cream into the melted carob, adding a sufficient amount to give a thick coating consistency. Use at once.

CAROB MILK COATING

Blend some milk into the melted carob in place of cream, again adding a sufficient amount to obtain the correct coating consistency.

CAROB AND VANILLA CREAM SAUCE

This thick and creamy sauce is delicious served warm over vanilla ice cream.

Imperial (Metric)	American
¼ pint (140ml) single cream	⅔ cupful light cream
1 vanilla pod, split lengthways	1 vanilla bean, split lengthways
1 x 2½oz (75g) carob bar	1 x 2½ ounce carob bar

1. Place the cream and vanilla pod in a saucepan and heat to just below boiling point. Cover the saucepan with a lid and set aside to infuse for about 15 minutes, so that the flavour of the vanilla pod penetrates the cream. Remove the vanilla pod after the infusion time, then re-heat the cream to simmering point.

2. Break the carob bar into pieces and place in a heat-resistant bowl. Set the bowl over a saucepan of gently simmering water, to melt the carob. When melted, add the infused cream a little at a time, blending to a smooth, thick sauce. Retain the sauce over the hot water to keep warm until ready to serve.

CAROB AND ORANGE CREAM SAUCE

The freshly grated zest of an orange is used to flavour this sauce which again makes an ideal accompaniment to ice cream.

Imperial (Metric)   **American**
¼ pint (140 ml) single cream   ⅔ cupful light cream
Finely grated zest of 1 orange   Finely grated zest of 1 orange
1 x 2½ oz (75 g) carob bar   1 x 2½ ounce carob bar

1. Scald the cream in a saucepan, then remove from the heat and stir in the finely grated orange zest.

2. Melt the carob bar over hot water, as above, then add the orange zest flavoured cream, blending to a smooth, thick sauce. Retain the cream over the hot water to keep warm until required.

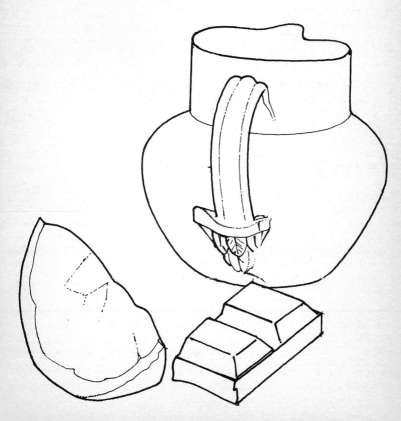

MOCHA CREAM SAUCE

The flavours of carob, vanilla and decaffeinated coffee are combined to make this mocha sauce.

Imperial (Metric)	American
¼ pint (140ml) single cream	⅔ cupful light cream
1 vanilla pod, split lengthways	1 vanilla bean, split lengthways
1 dessertspoonful decaffeinated coffee	2 teaspoonsful decaffeinated coffee
1 dessertspoonful light Muscovado sugar	2 teaspoonsful light Muscovado sugar
1 tablespoonful boiling water	1 tablespoonful boiling water
1 x 2½oz (75g) carob bar	1 x 2½ ounce carob bar

1. Heat the cream and vanilla pod to boiling point, then cover and set aside to infuse for about 15 minutes. Remove the vanilla pod after the infusion time, then re-heat the cream to simmering point.

2. Mix the decaffeinated coffee and Muscovado sugar together, then dissolve in the boiling water to make a concentrated coffee.

3. Break the carob bar into pieces and place in a heat-resistant bowl, together with the concentrated coffee. Set the bowl over a saucepan of gently simmering water, until the carob and coffee are melted to a smooth paste.

4. Gradually add the infused cream to the carob and coffee mixture, blending to a smooth sauce. Retain the sauce over the hot water to keep warm until ready to serve.

VANILLA AND MUSCOVADO CUSTARD SAUCE

A delicious custard sauce, flavoured with vanilla and sweetened with Muscovado sugar – an ideal accompaniment to hot puddings.

Imperial (Metric)	American
¾ pint (425 ml) milk	2 cupsful milk
1 vanilla pod, split lengthways	1 vanilla bean, split lengthways
4 egg yolks	4 egg yolks
2½ oz (75 g) light Muscovado sugar	½ cupful light Muscovado sugar

1. Place the milk and vanilla pod in a saucepan and bring to the boil. Remove from the heat, cover, and set aside to infuse for about 15 minutes. Remove the vanilla pod after the infusion time and re-heat the milk to simmering point.

2. Whisk the egg yolks and Muscovado sugar together until thick and creamy. Now slowly pour the vanilla-flavoured milk onto the egg mixture, in a thin stream, stirring constantly as the eggs are slowly warmed by the hot milk.

3. Pour into a heavy-based saucepan and allow to thicken very gradually, over a gentle heat, without allowing to boil. Stir the mixture continuously with a wooden spoon and remove from the heat when it has thickened sufficiently to coat the back of the spoon. This will take about 10 minutes. (The custard must not be allowed to come anywhere near to boiling point, or else the eggs will curdle.)

4. Strain the custard into a warmed serving jug and serve at once. If the custard is not to be used immediately, keep warm by setting over a saucepan of gently simmering water, or in the top of a double boiler.

CAROB LEAVES

Method 1:

Imperial (Metric)   **American**
1 x 2½oz (75g) carob bar   1 x 2½ ounce carob bar

1. Melt the carob in a heat-resistant bowl set over a saucepan of gently simmering water.

2. Spread the melted carob fairly thickly onto a sheet of waxed paper, spreading evenly with a palette knife.

3. When almost set, mark the carob into leaf shapes, using a sharp knife or decorative cutter.

4. When completely set, peel the leaf shapes off the waxed paper and use for decorating cakes, ice creams, etc.

Method 2:

Imperial (Metric)   **American**
1 x 2½oz (75g) carob bar   1 x 2½ ounce carob bar
Glossy leaves   Glossy leaves

1. Melt the carob in a heat-resistant bowl set over a saucepan of gently simmering water.

2. Collect some thick, glossy leaves such as rose or camellia, with distinctive veins. Wash thoroughly.

3. Spread the melted carob over the glossy side of the leaves, making sure that they are fully coated.

4. Leave until thoroughly set, then very carefully peel off the leaves. The original leaf veins will now have been transposed onto the carob leaves, making a very attractive decoration for cakes and desserts.

VANILLA SUGAR

To obtain vanilla sugar, place a whole vanilla pod (vanilla bean) in a covered jar of raw cane sugar (Demerara and Muscovado are ideal), and leave to stand for about 2 weeks before using. During this time, the sugar will become saturated with the flavour of the vanilla pod. Leave the pod in the jar of sugar, keeping tightly covered to retain the flavour, and use as required.

This sugar is particularly good in carob cakes – the natural vanilla flavour combines especially well with that of carob.

INDEX